This is an important book. Young readers will experience what it's like in a youth custody center—from the first moment of admission to the terrible isolation and fear of spending long days and nights behind bars. But perhaps the book is even more important for parents. This book might just save your kids.

—Barry Bowman, writer and broadcaster, Victoria

The book is one-of-a-kind. No one else has ever written about the experiences from a juvenile detention centre. With his ambition and patience Cruse has created a resource, with considerable understanding for anyone whose life is affected by troubled youth.

—Ned Powers, *The StarPhoenix*, Saskatoon

As a parent, my gut tightened in knots when reading about a young man arriving in handcuffs and shackles at juvie . . . . Still, there is the sound of triumph in Gord's book, the triumph of a "firm but fair" man who listened without judging.

—Reverend Walter Donald,
president, BC Association of Police Boards

It's about time something like this has been written.

—Rick, resident, 1980s

Early intervention in troubled kids' lives is the key . . . kids don't suddenly become killers at the age of 13.

—Chuck Cadman, former MP Surrey North

Juvie: Inside Canada's Youth Jails

GORDON CRUSE

JUVIE

Inside Canada's Youth Jails

GORDON CRUSE

Library and Archives Canada Cataloguing in Publication

Cruse, Gordon, 1942–
Juvie : inside Canada's youth jails / Gordon Cruse.

ISBN 978-1-894694-43-8
ISBN 1-894694-43-0

1. Juvenile justice, Administration of—British Columbia. 2. Juvenile detention homes—British Columbia. 3. Juvenile delinquents—British Columbia. I. Title.

HV9108.C78 2006   364.3609711   C2006-906363-X

Editors: Fernanda Vivieros, Beth Grabham, Graham Hayman
Book and back cover design: Laura Kinder
Front Cover design: Wesley Fok
First Printing: January 2007
Printed in Canada

Granville Island Publishing
212 – 1656 Duranleau
Vancouver, BC V6H 3S4
Tel: (604) 688-0320
info@GranvilleIslandPublishing.com
www.GranvilleIslandPublishing.com

Front cover photograph by Roland Dawkins
Back cover: photographer unknown
Page 53 top and page 54 middle: photographers unknown
Rest of the photos in this section by Gordon Cruse
Photo of author: Art Holbrook

IN MEMORY OF CHUCK CADMAN

For the kids

CONTENTS

RAW VOICES: POETRY & PROSE

Many of my fellow staff and colleagues who work with troubled kids across this country have made helpful connections with the kids in our centres, and these relationships have been, not surprisingly, mutually beneficial.

The letters on the 'Raw Voices' pages throughout this book are a few of the dozens I have received and continue to receive from Juvie residents over the years. They have a common theme of reaching out for a real connection.

Foreword

Gordon Cruse is a communicator. I guess we both learned the art of communication when we were brash radio disc jockeys together over forty years ago. He was moving to evenings at CFQC in Saskatoon and had the dispiriting charge of teaching me the ropes when I joined as the new all-night guy on *The Waxworks*. There were a lot of technical things and routines to remember, or so it seemed to a neophyte trainee such as me. But it was evident even back then that his particular style of easygoing patience and quiet resolve made the task quite painless—for both of us.

I stayed in radio for the next thirty-five years while Gord moved on. Evidently there was something else out there he was searching for and finally, after hiking the world twice, he found it. His communication skills, learned those many years ago behind a microphone, were put to use, this time behind bars as a supervisor in B.C.'s youth justice system.

Gord developed a singular talent for connecting with troubled teens. That same sincere and patient determination, that quiet understanding, allowed Gord the opportunity to communicate with these kids. Street-wise kids can instinctively smell phony but they opened up to him. They knew he cared. They trusted him. And he never betrayed that trust. And so began a career that spanned more years on the line face-to-face with troubled kids than most line staff.

Juvie is the first book of its kind. It's the first real ground-level look at B.C.'s youth custody system from the point of view of someone who worked up front and on the line every day. (It should be noted that Gord never took a sick day in over twenty-six years!) So why hasn't a book like this been written before? Because few can claim the experience of working so many years in such close proximity to juvenile killers, thieves and other violent offenders.

Few can claim the bonds that were forged for so many years after the kids got back on the street and either re-offended or went straight. Few could remark to so many troubled kids that he knew their parents when they were under his watch a generation earlier. This is not to say that scores of dedicated supervisors in the system didn't develop the same relationships or didn't have the same commitment to their jobs. It's simply that Gord Cruse did it among the longest and, for so many that have come and gone, is perhaps the best remembered. To some, he is a legend. His reputation for strict, yet fair cooperation, his playful kidding and constant unconditional understanding of those who rarely got a chance to just feel someone may actually be listening to them, is renowned.

Gordon Cruse has a lot to say about B.C.'s youth justice system and he doesn't pull any punches. He's been a keen observer of the fairness as well as the injustice from the line duty members all the way up to the judges. He's outspoken and honestly still cares about how the system works and could work better.

This is an important book. To both young readers who will experience what it's like from the first moment of admission to the terrible isolation and fear of spending long days and nights behind bars. It's even more important for you parents. This book might just save your kid.

   —Barry Bowman
    January 2006

Recognition & Appreciation

I wish to express my appreciation and recognition:

• For the men and women whose clearly-expressed opinions during personal conversations with me in locations from St. John's, Newfoundland and Hartford, Connecticut to North Battleford, Saskatchewan, Seattle, Washington and Perth, Australia confirmed my own thoughts about my work with youth.

• For my broadcasting friends in Canada and England whose talents and zest for life influenced and encouraged a quiet, shy young man during the early years of my working life.

• For my high school and university friends whose critical support has shaped a better me, and whose opinions I continue to value.

• For the women and men at Victoria's Youth Custody Centre for their ongoing respect and the fun they brought into our work, and for all the men and women who work in the connected fields of youth care whose paths crossed mine in the adventure.

• For my extended family whose love and support is the anchor for my life.

• For my parents, Gladys and Freddie, always there.

• For Bob, a fun-loving brother, and a friend.

• For my grandsons Ricky and Corey—how rich a gift they are in the autumn of my life.

• For the families of young offenders who have shared their lives and their feelings with me.

• For the young offenders whose lives have touched me personally.

- For the young offenders who are no longer with us.
- For senator and former Vancouver mayor Larry Campbell's succint advice to our corrections officer training class when he was chief coronor for British Columbia – keep a notebook. *Juvie* is my notebook. Thank you Mr. Campbell.
- For all the men and women whose textured and insightful comments enrich this book with their inclusion.
- And a special thank you to Natalie for her computer skills, hours of patience and wisdom shared in the shaping of this work, and her husband Cory for his humour and perceptive insights about kids.

Introduction

From 1976 to 2002, I worked face-to-face with young offenders at the Victoria Youth Custody Centre in Victoria, British Columbia. Twenty-six years on the line is quite exceptional. My experience spanned three major federal legal acts—from the old Juvenile Delinquents Act to the Young Offenders Act to today's Youth Criminal Justice Act. I was also involved at a local chapter of Big Brothers in 1969 and served as a probation sponsor for family court. Along with being a foster parent for the British Columbia government since 1973, I believe these decades of experience with troubled youth created a unique career that has given me a perspective worth sharing in this book.

My education included two years of pre-med at the University of Saskatchewan in the early sixties. Then broadcasting consumed a fourteen-year period in my life after I began work as an announcer at CFQC Radio in Saskatoon while attending university. Six years at CFQC was followed by a one-year stint as a rock n' roll disc jockey and newsman on Radio Caroline, the first British offshore pirate radio station! In 1969, I returned to Canada and worked at CFAX Radio in Victoria as a music director and operations manager until 1974 when I began my work with young offenders.

During my career at the custody centre, I completed courses in conflict resolution, the female offender, the mentally disordered young offender, the adolescent sex offender, management, the Young Offenders Act and the Youth Criminal Justice Act among others at the Justice Institute of British Columbia, Simon Fraser University,

University of British Columbia and the University of Victoria.

If we expect youth to be accountable for their actions, we must demonstrate it ourselves. As a broadcaster, I was taught how to lift the words off paper, do the work for the listener and tell the story. Communicating is at the heart of working with teens. We must communicate with control and with compassion, and judge the crime, not its perpetrator. My time in pre-med showed me that I wanted the people, not the science, in my life. My broadcasting years were the seasoning that I needed to work successfully with rowdy and emotional kids. I developed patience and people skills from learning how to interview people, and ad-libbing on air taught me how to respond when put on the spot. Twenty-six years working eyeball-to-eyeball with kids exhibiting some of the worst behaviours one can imagine gave me a perspective that few people have experienced.

I've made many observations from my career as a youth corrections officer. Children learn what they live, making one child's idea of what a 'normal' life is, appear to us as abusive, chaotic, criminal, dysfunctional and not acceptable in the societal norm. Unfortunately the long and convoluted path to realigning a child's unbalanced life usually has to start once a kid has broken the law after many years of dealing with his or her own personal chaos.

In a custodial setting of a juvenile detention centre, or 'Juvie,' the youth's emotional confusion usually manifests in bizarre behaviours, rule-breaking, defensive and belligerent attitudes, violence, suicide attempts or a sour outlook on life. Because there is a microcosm of teenage society packed into the small building of a youth custody centre, the full run of youths' emotions and life's battles are concentrated in the day-to-day routine. Staff see the kids daily, face-to-face, so they become the most consistent adult figures in their lives—perhaps more consistent than any before.

The opinions of Juvie staff have also shaped this book, which I hope will be a valuable resource for teens, parents, caregivers and youth justice workers. I am sharing these stories and opinions to increase public understanding of the youth justice system, to spark different attitudes concerning treatment, to recognize those professionals who worked with young offenders, and to promote respect and acceptance as a community's responsibility towards kids who are not generally accepted or wanted.

I have found that because I have worked with very disturbed girls and boys for many years, I am suddenly an 'expert' on kids and parenting. No way! What I can simply offer parents is many years' worth of experience based on what I have seen works and doesn't work. Every adult who is responsible for a child learns from the experience of others. As a parent, I know we can't think of everything ourselves so we need all the information we can gather.

I have been one of those fortunate people who found a fulfilling vocation. My job satisfaction came from the communication I established with troubled kids and by showing them respectful ways to treat people. I believe my ability to communicate and be helpful to young people is my gift, with no ulterior motives or hidden agendas. Sometimes I felt as though I was being selfish because I was satisfying my need to communicate on a daily basis. This charged my emotional batteries and I was able to give back more than I had received. During my career as a youth correctional officer, it was those friendships with the kids that enriched my life and balanced out many of the stresses of working with really troubled kids. I also enjoyed working with most of the men and women who were my peers. I had no ulcers, no high blood pressure and no regrets!

As my grandmother once said, "An ounce of prevention is worth a pound of cure," and this applies today to all young people, offenders or not. I firmly believe that parents, caregivers and governments should vigorously pursue intervention and prevention programs when children are at an early age in order to steer them away from the dangerous side roads of life they will inevitably encounter as they get older.

I am honoured that two ex-residents have named their children after me. To have that kind of a legacy is to be recognized and appreciated in the greatest way. I am now retired. I live in Victoria where I enjoy the company of a wonderful lady friend, my grandsons Ricky and Corey, family, friends, the ongoing friendships with many ex-residents and restoring old cars and young hearts!

I'd like to share two moments, one with my father and one with my grandsons which greatly influenced my job at Juvie. One Halloween, my father had left some candy in a bowl on our front porch because we weren't going to be home for the trick-or-treaters. I said, "But one kid will take it all!" My dad peered inside my fourteen-year-old head and said, "They'll share." My father's sense of trust and his positive attitude stayed with me throughout my life.

Many years later, during the Christmas holidays, I took my two grandsons on a tour of Juvie. They had been busting with curiosity about where I worked, and wanted to give the residents some oranges and little chocolates. Outside on the front step afterwards, nine-year-old Corey said, "They did bad things, didn't they Grandpa Gord?"

"Yes, Corey, they did," I said.

His older brother, Ricky, looked at me with the innocent wisdom and trust borne of eleven years life experience and said, "But they have good hearts."

On my last day of work at Juvie, I remember my feelings slipped silently and sadly from somewhere inside me as I was overwhelmed with the generations of memories as I took a final look down the East Wing. How many thousands of young offenders had I met who tested and trampled the theories of a thousand psychologists, psychiatrists, counsellors, child care workers, behaviourists, probation officers, professors, parents and starry-eyed staff with their energetic attitudes, boisterousness and sheer against-the-grain rebelliousness? On this last shift at Victoria's Youth Custody Centre, the memories on my cheeks marked the passing of so many troubled pasts, tortured emotions, seething anger, and bubbling, emotional cauldrons—a microcosm of our communities' injustices that were locked in an artificial setting. What an amazing quarter-century!

—Gordon Cruse

PART ONE   The Kids

Chapter 1   The Circle Game

"Admissions."

The greeting from Admissions Officer 'Dave' sounds almost routine.

"One on the way from Saanich . . . first time . . . very distraught."

Dave prepares to admit a 14-year-old boy. He readies the admission book, a personal effects sheet, the rationale for admission form, a towel stamped with Government of British Columbia, some Juvie sweats and disinfecting shampoo.

The kid arrives in handcuffs and shackles. Have you ever seen a kid in cuffs and shackles? Even after twenty-six years, it still affects me. The cuffs and shackles come off, the police sign our forms and leave. The kid sits slouched in the chair as the admission procedure begins.

"Name . . . age . . . address . . . live with your parents?"

So what happens? Your child is in jail! The sickening feeling in your gut when the phone rings at four in the morning and the authoritative voice on the other end asks, "Is this Mr./Mrs—?"

"Yes" you reply.

"My name is Officer — of — Police. Do you have a son named — ?"

"Yes."

You speak through emotionally wrenched vocal cords.

"Your son has been arrested and is being detained at the police station."

The butterflies in your stomach are more like pterodactyls as your anxiety races your car to the police station. *What's happened? He was in his room when we went to bed. How can this be?*

Pressing the bell at the police station at this hour activates a disembodied voice—polite, business-like and intimidating—instructing you to enter and please wait . . . an officer will attend momentarily. The charge is assault causing bodily harm, resulting in emergency treatment for the victim — your son was involved. Because of the seriousness of the incident, your son will be taken to the Youth Custody Centre. The police explain to you that because this is the weekend and there are no courts sitting, your son will appear before a justice of the peace. Police recommendation is that he be held in custody until Monday morning, when he will appear before a judge. At that time, the judge will decide either to remand your son into the community on his own recognizance, or to remand him in custody.

The police allow you a few minutes with your son, and what a sad and shocking sight he is. Blood spatters his t-shirt, his hands are cuffed behind his back, his legs are in shackles, and he is sitting, head bowed, in a stark concrete room on a bench bolted to the wall. But it's when he raises his head as you enter, and he can't quite look you in the eye that you really see his pain and shame and fear. And you haven't seen tears like these since he was a little boy.

Hundreds of these scenarios pass through my mind as I think of all the kids I've known over the years, each of whom trembled their fearful way through this experience. I feel a twinge of their heartache. There but for the grace of God . . .

Admission to a maximum security youth custody centre is a frightening, intimidating and humiliating experience. A police officer escorts the 'prisoner' (humiliating in itself) from the police car to the admissions door of the centre. At four in the morning, the centre is quiet and looming. Two staff members take legal possession of the young offender from the arresting officers with signatures on the appropriate paperwork. The police leave after removing the shackles and handcuffs and the admission procedure begins.

For the next 45 to 50 minutes, questions are asked of the youth to determine name, age, address, physical description, medical needs and answers to questions—have parents been notified, do you have a social worker, a probation officer, a lawyer, a contact in case of emergency, etc.

If a child appears to be under the influence of any drug or alcohol, or is sick, or there is a suspicion of any sort of abnormality, staff will not accept the child until he or she has been checked by a doctor. All clothing is listed and described by a staff member as the young person hands his or her belongings to a second officer. One staff member visually checks the youth as the clothing items are removed, and the youth is asked to turn around as the officer visually checks for symptoms of disease, cuts, bruises, abrasion or injuries/abnormalities of any kind. Body piercing or tattoos are also recorded. Out of the child's sight, but in sight of the search officer, a second staff member observes the strip search procedure, and provides back-up and protection for the officer conducting the search. Female staff members conduct the searches on female admissions while male staff members are responsible for strip-searching male admissions. This is the most respectful and least embarrassing way to conduct a very necessary part of the admissions protocol.

We are also checking for contraband which could be used to

harm staff members or other residents. Contraband can include drugs, weapons or anything else which could be harmful to any person in the centre, or which could interfere with the safety and security of the centre. Contraband is seized and recorded; it may be needed at a later time for a court-related situation. After the resident is given clothing, disinfecting shampoo, soap and a towel, he or she must take a shower before being placed in a room. Welcome to Juvie.

Youth incarceration in Victoria took place at 1125 Pembroke Street from 1963 until 2002. At a cost of $93,000 for construction, the City of Victoria provided 'youth lock-up' at this address until 1974, when the Ministry of the Attorney General took over the supervision of youth in custody. Originally the site was referred to as the Juvenile Detention Home, then later as the Youth Detention Centre. With the incorporation of the Young Offenders Act in 1984, the centre became known as the Victoria Youth Custody Centre (VYCC) and was designated a maximum-security jail for young offenders. At this time, there were twenty beds at the VYCC, and at closing time in June of 2002 there were forty-four beds, although at times we slept as many as fifty-six kids in the building.

When I started working at Juvie in 1976, a full house was ten or twelve kids. There were very few girls admitted in those days, and administration would only call in a female officer if there were girls in residence. A majority of the men on staff were ex-military officers at the time, and because there was no formal structure of authority we tended to lean towards the military style of governance. A few times I worked several days in a row with no kids at all in the building, so we did a lot of painting and cleaning!

In the early years of my tenure at Juvie, there were no programs. There was a television set on each wing and a basketball hoop in the seventy-five foot square concrete courtyard, and that was it! The kids watched television, played cards, and eight times a day enjoyed a smoke. I was nervous the first time I had to hand out cigarettes! I walked into the East TV room with an armload of cigarette packs each marked with a kid's name to hand out, and I didn't even know their names—that was a fun time!

Housing young offenders in a youth centre is a delicate process. Resident placement in the old centre on Pembroke Street meant East Wing or West Wing. East Wing contained nine rooms, five single and four double. West Wing had seven rooms, two double and five single. All boys went automatically to the East Wing and all girls to the West Wing, except when the number of boys exceeded the thirteen spots that the East Wing would hold and then the West Wing would become co-ed to receive the overflow.

Staff took great care to select the boys who would be allowed residency on the West Wing with the girls, usually choosing the lads who were the best behaved with the females. You're allowed to arrive at Juvie pregnant, but you're not allowed to become pregnant while you're there! Sometimes it didn't matter how many doors you locked. Teenagers are driven by their hormones and even though staff made every effort to keep things appropriate between the boys and girls, I'm sure there were things happening between them that even the staff didn't know about.

The new VYCC building located at 94 Talcott Road opened as a maximum-security youth facility in June of 2002. There are forty-eight beds in the facility with expansion to a maximum of sixty beds possible. Program and resident living buildings border a grassy outdoor courtyard. There are four living units with two designated as open custody and two as closed custody. One of the closed custody units handles special-needs kids while the other houses general remand and sentenced kids. Closed custody is co-ed, housing girls and boys twelve to seventeen years of age.

The City of Victoria ran the old centre from its opening in 1963 to 1974 when the Youth Detention Centre was turned over to the provincial government, and placed under the Attorney General's Ministry. Employees are BCGEU (British Columbia Government Employees Union) members and government employees. There were only two things that bothered me about being an employee at the centre. I had to belong to a union, and I was working for the government. Still, I can honestly say I was not harmed by either one over the years! I also made a choice about my career path. I stayed on the line with the kids. Only once did I enter management when I was asked by the director at the time to be a shift supervisor. I worked in this position for about 15 months in 1983-84. I did it adequately, made some mistakes, but passed the position on because I really was not interested in middle management. This is not to negate or denigrate management positions or the people in them. Management is a necessary part of any organization, and I always tried to support and help the people holding these positions of authority. However, my focus was always on the kids.

Stories that you will read in the chapters ahead are from memory and from several dozen letters received since 1976. These stories fill these pages with laughter, anger, sadness, hope, violence, birth, death, bureaucracy, freedom, escape, suicide, honour, shame, riots and birthday cakes. They will move you, entertain you and, most of all, reveal to you the inside of Juvie. All of the stories are true. This book is written to educate, to increase knowledge and understanding, to communicate, to warn, to explain and to offer suggestions, ideas, alternatives and perhaps catalyze a fresh approach or a new idea in how we care for a valuable and irreplaceable part of our society—our children.

I will also introduce you to a diverse group of professionals and institutional settings I have encountered over my career in the youth justice system. I've toured detention centres from Newfoundland to Australia, met with judges, social workers, inmates and probation officers, and worked with hundreds of kids throughout my long career as a youth supervisor. I hope this book offers an insider's perspective about some of what happens when children live apart from their families and the life experiences that brought these young offenders before the law. I will always respect the oath of confidentiality to which I swore when I was hired. I know and knew these young people, and respect their right to remain anonymous. It is the teaching value of their experiences which brings them onto these pages.

RAW VOICES I

"Ned"

Ned sent me a note while he was attending a program at the old House of Concorde run by the Salvation Army in Langley, near Vancouver. This was a court-ordered attendance program, supervised by probation officers designed to modify kids' behaviour while they were in a live-in residential setting. It was the early 1980s.

I hate this place everyone seems to pick on me, the big guys that is. On Sunday I am going home for two days, which will be nice. I really hate this place because it's rotten, lousy, and it stinks. The other night I had a fight, it wasn't too bad I won but I still hate it.

It really bugs me being in this place. I don't feel like I'm me, I feel like I'm someone else. I really hate myself. I phoned home today, no one was home but my dad. We talked for a while and he started crying. It makes me feel so bad when I think how badly I've hurt them I almost feel like killing myself. Well bed time.

Chapter 2 David

I met David in the summer of 1980. As part of the line staff at the Victoria Youth Custody Centre, we supervised residents from the time they got up in the morning until we put them in their rooms at night. When the staff admitted David he was assigned to the West Wing, where I was working that day. At this time, the West Wing housed both boys and girls so we really had to be on our toes when we oversaw this bunch. A blond-haired, blue-eyed seventeen-year-old, David quickly caught the eyes of the girls on the wing. Although full of mischief and energy that required staff to keep a close eye on him, David respected the no-contact rule between the boys and girls.

One day during David's incarceration, we had the residents from the West Wing out in the courtyard for some fresh air and social interaction with the kids from the East Wing. The recreation area was basically a seventy-five square-foot concrete sandbox with twenty-foot-high walls. It wasn't the most attractive environment, but it was way ahead of the alternative—the kids' six-by-eight-foot concrete-walled rooms. At the end of recreation time, David got into a fight with one of the boys on his wing so I sent him to his room for a time-out. In order to leave the recreation area to lock David into his cell, I had to call for staff to watch the other eight or ten residents. As I waited for the backup to arrive and just after David was out of my sight, I heard a loud whoosh and some swearing from the hallway. By the time I reached David, he had emptied the fire extinguisher in the hallway. I took it from him and placed him in his room.

As I checked on David frequently over the next several hours, I could see that he was still angry. The tight leash David held on his frustrations with his family and his dealings with the law was apparent—the fight and the extinguisher incident had merely been his way of dealing with his emotions. As his rage simmered, I was able to talk to him and explain the consequences of his behaviour. This disciplinary exchange proved to be the catalyst for our friendship. I was able to establish some ground rules for our conversations which gave him the opportunity to talk about his feelings openly.

Fights and destructive behaviour are cries for help. Juvie is a place where these kids have to start acknowledging their troubled past and current problems, while at the same time dealing with the loss of their freedom. Often their emotions explode because they just don't know how to cope with their pain and frustration. Whenever I had to approach the kids, I felt it was important to simply be open, honest and non-judgmental—sometimes just by listening I could help untangle their emotional confusion. The most frequent comment from the kids about this process was, "You don't need to fix it, just listen to me!" This was the situation with David. By promising him whatever was said would stay between us, he felt comfortable in sharing his feelings about his family life with me.

Over the following year, David was released and re-admitted several times, as is the case with some teenagers in Juvie. We got to know each other as David made his re-appearances during the fall and winter of 1980/1981. Aboveboard interactions between staff and residents were maintained in order to protect the boundaries between the staff and the young residents in our care. Staff kept tabs on the residents' behaviour while the residents observed staff to see if they could be counted on to stick to their word. Credibility was earned when each side lived up to the other's expectations. Respect is the key to interactions with troubled kids; if staff members carry an agenda, the kids figure that out very quickly. Apparently I passed the test with David, who decided that I was firm and fair. He liked that, as he told me later.

Part of the job for staff at Juvie was to lead a group of kids in a work crew to clean the building. Mops, pails, rags and cleaner, look out washroom, here we come! Most kids chose to be in the work crew since the alternative was to sit by themselves in their rooms for that ninety-minute program period. The work crew program was one way to encourage meaningful conversations among staff and residents and a good way to get them to know one another. With mop or toilet brush in hand, male and female residents talked about religion, parents, discipline, girlfriends or boyfriends. In particular, David was one work crew kid who took part in and benefited from this social atmosphere that encouraged words rather than punches.

This schedule illustrates a typical weekday at the centre:

08:00   The kids are awakened whereupon they complete quick
         chores and wash up for breakfast
08:30   Breakfast is served
09:00   Programs begin: school, arts and crafts, woodworking
12:00   Lunch is served
13:00   Programs continue
16:00   Leisure time spent in the living units or outdoor courtyard
17:00   Dinner is served

17:45   Staff Break

18:30   Evening programs: arts and crafts, board games, gym or
          outdoor courtyard

20:00   Leisure time spent watching television, reading, playing
          in outdoor courtyard, visits (family)

21:30   Kids returned to their rooms for the night

22:00   Higher-level residents returned to their rooms for the night

At various times during the day, residents are locked in their rooms
in order for staff members to take a lunch break and conduct
brief shift changes. Some staff members are on eight-hour shifts
while others work a twelve-hour shift. Weekend schedules are less
structured. Arts and craft activities are available Saturday until 3
pm and movies are shown Friday, Saturday and Sunday evenings
from 7 to 9 pm. On Sundays after lunch, a spirituality program is
offered to the residents, with music and refreshments included in
this optional program. Drug and alcohol counseling discussion
groups are sometimes available through a program hosted by
recovering alcoholics and drug addicts.

In early 1981 I was in the process of re-shingling the roof of
my house. At the time, David was out of VYCC, so he used to
make his way to my place, where he would sit on the roof and
talk with me. Our chats were sometimes humorous, often serious,
and sometimes even tearful. Because of the twenty-kilometre
drive back to his home, David would sometimes, with his parents'
permission, stay for supper and crash on my couch.

"You don't nag or order me around," said David.

"So who does?" I asked.

"My parents!" was his reply. Although David had been in and
out of Juvie, he was still a typical teenager, annoyed with his mom

and dad's ordinary, disciplined and loving parenting.

In early August of that same year, I took my foster son and his friends camping at a small lake situated north of Victoria. After the kids fell asleep, I stayed up with the dwindling campfire, watching the scarlet sunset dance on the water. Later, in my tent, I found myself lying awake thinking about David. I hadn't seen him for a few weeks and was concerned with how he was doing. A couple of nights later we returned to Victoria and there was a phone message waiting for me from David's father. David was dead. He had been in a serious car accident. His car had rolled over the same night I had been awake thinking about him at the campsite. His dad told me that during those last days in the hospital, David—severely injured—had been asking for me.

The memorial service for David was held at a little chapel near the Jubilee Hospital in Victoria. Still in operation, the chapel is almost hidden by the towering brick walls of the hospital's new additions. Whenever I walk past the old chapel, the memory of David's bright, mischievous and short life saddens me and I recall how I shook when I delivered a brief eulogy at his parents' request at his memorial service all those years ago. A few months after his death his family sent a picture of David to me along with a letter that read, "We hope to see you again, Gordon, and will always remember you for your trust and kindness to David." David's journey in life was short. He had many friends, loving parents, a brother, a girlfriend and many adventures. I can't even remember what he was in Juvie for—his brushes with the law were more a measure of his spirit than an indicator of a lifestyle.

Chapter 3   The Adoptee

Introducing a teenager to his birth mother was one of the most emotional and momentous occasions I experienced in twenty-six years of highs and lows working in a youth centre. Sometimes when I worked with a kid, I would form an attachment without even realizing it was happening.

It was the autumn of 1993 and I had just returned from a wonderful holiday in Connecticut. The seasonal colours on the Eastern seaboard were stunning as nature prepared the landscape for winter and I enjoyed time spent visiting with an old school friend. Friendship means a great deal to me, so reuniting with my old buddy was a wonderful occasion. During my stay, I was fortunate to be able to tour the Long Lane School, a youth centre nestled in the green hills north of Hartford.

By the time I returned to work, I was refreshed, energized and ready for all the situations I might encounter. It was at this time that I met Bill, who was on remand. He had been with a friend when he found a loonie—a one-dollar coin—on the sidewalk. The friend had been putting on his jacket and apparently the coin had dropped out of a pocket. The friend later accused Bill of taking the money and the police arrested Bill and parked him in Juvie while the youth justice system conducted this very crucial 'investigation' into Bill's alleged crime.

As Bill waited for the cops, lawyers and judge to figure out if he was a hardcore young offender needing punishment, he adjusted to life inside Juvie. Bill quietly worked, scrubbing sinks and cleaning urinals without complaint. As he got used to me supervising the work crew, he started to open up and tell me his story.

Our work crew conversations continued over the next two months while Bill was at Juvie. Regularly after lock-down we would sit on the floor of his room for an 'open doorway talk.' I would sit on the floor in his room's doorway and listen. Sitting on the floor with the kids was one way for me to mitigate the image of authority held by staff. Also, sitting in the doorway was a way of protecting my position so that other staff could observe me easily and know that I was just there to provide a sympathetic ear for the kids.

Our conversations were at times childish, humorous, silly and intellectual, but always respectful. Many times Bill would ask about my values and what I thought of certain people's behaviour and the little things that pissed him off. Because I told Bill—and the other kids—during our open-doorway sessions that I wasn't a blabbermouth and would keep their words confidential, Bill would feel comfortable in revealing some of the personal feelings he kept hidden from others most of the time.

Two months after being admitted, Bill was released. He went to court and stood before the judge, anxious to hear of his fate. The judge tore a strip off every official in the courtroom and dismissed the charges against Bill. Finally, freedom! Like most kids about to step back on the 'outs,' Bill was full of mixed emotions: the excitement of anticipating freedom; anxiety over what would happen to him; and of course, relief to know that he would soon see his friends and family again.

About a week after his release, I came out of work after day shift, and there, standing on the sidewalk, was Bill and his adoptive mother. They had come to Victoria to say hello and have a visit with me. Bill asked if we could continue our friendship, which we did.

Two years later, Bill came to stay with me as a boarder with the permission of his social worker and his probation officer. On the day we were moving him into my home, he asked a question right out of the blue. "Will you help me find my birth parents?" He was an adult, eighteen years old now, and wanted some answers about his birth parents. I spoke with his adoptive mother first to ask for her permission. She was very supportive, but, like me, she didn't really know how to begin the search for his birth parents.

My first step was a trip to the library to begin my search for his biological parents. No luck. Next, I went to friends who had contacts, and bingo! I had an address, name, and phone number. His birth mom was living in the Lower Mainland, just a ninety-minute ferry ride and one-hour drive from Victoria. The search for Bill's birth mother had succeeded so quickly that I became apprehensive. Was this the proper approach? Should I phone the woman first? Or should I hand this over to an agency?

I sought advice from an agency that specialized in locating birth parents. The woman at the agency was a gem. She was helpful, understanding and entirely trustworthy. After some discussion, we decided that she and I would call the birth mother on Bill's behalf.

The first phone call was very emotional. Bill's birth mother cried—she had believed that her son was dead. He was born with a chronic disease and she had given him up for adoption, later hearing that he had died when he was eight. As her tears subsided, I described Bill's personality and physical appearance, and she was convinced he was her biological son. Now there was no holding her back from seeing her son again. We made arrangements for her to arrive at my house with her daughter— Bill's biological sister—later that day. Bill was out back, working on my new garage roof when the doorbell rang. I opened the door to greet his birth mother, who was whirling with excitement.

"Where is he?" she asked.

"Out back," I replied.

Zoom! She headed right through the house and out to the backyard to see Bill sitting on the roof.

"Are you Bill?" she called up to him.

"Yes," he said, and jumped down from the roof.

Mother and son stood and looked at each other, eye to eye, for a moment, then grasped hands and hugged. What an incredible moment that was to watch the two of them reunite after so many years apart. Bill's sister was waiting in our living room and I watched as he went in and introduced himself to her. It was a dramatic 'real life' moment and I felt privileged to have been a part of this experience.

Bill's birth mom invited him back to her home, and over the next few days mother and son became reacquainted. He learned that she and his birth father had long been divorced, but coincidently she had been in touch with her ex-husband recently and so was able to supply Bill with contact information. Later that summer, Bill and I journeyed to Eastern Canada to meet him.

Since Bill rediscovered his birth family, his relationship with them has continued to grow despite lots of ups and downs as they struggle to resolve family issues. Years later, he was married in a beautiful outdoor ceremony with both his birth mother and his adoptive mother in attendance. Bill and I remain regularly in touch. We are into our second decade of friendship and his wife marvels at the duration and quality of our relationship.

RAW VOICES II

Poem: "Left as a Child"

Some thoughts in poetry from another resident, this material is from the mid-eighties:

Oh mother
Where are you now?
I'm all alone
You left me as a child
To make it on my own.

Dear father
You were never there
When I needed you
You left me as a child
What was I to do?

Just a child
Thrown
From home to home
A parent's love I've never known.

I've lived a life
Of hardships and pain
Misery
'Cause I never learned the things
That you were to teach me.

No!
It's not my fault
That my life
Turned out the way it did
For, I had no understanding
I was just a kid.

Chapter 4   Secrets, Blame and the Name Game

Kids are often as sick as their secrets—and they can carry their secrets around for a lifetime.

Stick Bug, Two-Tone and Dog Boy were the nicknames of real kids I knew at the Victoria Youth Custody Centre. At fifteen, Stick Bug—nicknamed by one of our staff—was six-foot one and so skinny he had to run around in the shower to get wet! In the early eighties, many kids in the country were bleaching their hair and one of the first residents at VYCC to follow the trend was Two-Tone. Sometimes the nicknames were more personal. Names were often hurled from prejudicial, racial, ethnic and status quivers, and these venomous arrows were at the root of many an altercation.

One lad, whom I shall refer to as Dog Boy, may have never known he had a nickname. The nursing staff gave us the heads-up that we would be receiving a kid who needed some very special attention. Apparently this thirteen-year-old lived in a house with a large number of animals, and apparently the animals had received more attention than the children. So when Dog Boy was under stress he would get down on all fours and bark for attention. I only saw him do this one time while I was on shift but it was the most disturbing thing to see. He upset the other kids, who just backed away from him because they couldn't understand the situation— they saw how psychologically damaged he was and found no humour in taunting him with the usual bullying common among teenagers. As staff we were not set up to deal with him adequately and were at a loss as how to help the boy. Fortunately, his stay with us was brief and after only a few days he was removed from Juvie and placed elsewhere.

"I think I made my mom and dad break up!" Brady said to me one day, his voice choking with emotion. "I always heard them say my name when they were arguing."

The tears spilled from his dark eyes. I was affected—not many sixteen-year-olds cry in front of anyone. My relationship with Brady had grown over the few months he had been remanded to us. It was the mid-eighties and Juvie was still in the old VYCC building on Pembroke Street. On this particular summer afternoon, we were "circling the concrete sandbox"—in other words, walking the perimeter of the recreation area. These walks offered the kids an opportunity to have private conversations at Juvie without being overheard by other residents or staff. Brady told me he liked how I kept my mouth shut and just listened to him as we talked and walked. "The shrinks blab all my problems to everybody," he said.

That day, the mood in the courtyard was calm and relaxed as Brady and I circled while two additional staff members and I supervised a little over a dozen other residents. Brady told me his family was struggling financially. His dad had been laid off from his job and his mom was working part-time and caring for Brady's young siblings. His parents argued and eventually separated. As the eldest child, he felt guilty for costing his parents money to feed and clothe him. With intentions of easing the burden, Brady would stay away from home for days at a time so his parents would have one less mouth to feed. His absences would be the cause of further serious arguments whenever he returned home for clean clothes and to touch base with his brothers and sister. As he continued to lead the life of a runaway and a truant, Brady ran short of money. This led to crime, which in turn led him to Juvie.

As we circled, we talked about how he could find more productive ways of supporting his family (other than staying out of the house), of ways to change his behaviour, and the people and organizations he could turn to for assistance. He was at once angry, sad, ashamed and lonely, and it took some listening and talking on my part to help him express and understand what he was feeling. I was curious about his home life so I asked him to tell me specifically what made him think that he was the reason for his parents' separation. Brady couldn't give me a precise answer. It was just a feeling he had about them, he told me, even though his parents were still living together. The circling stopped at a very emotional point in our exchange and he turned his back to the other kids and faced me. The tears on his cheeks provided the cue I needed to return him to his room.

As I opened the door to his room Brady stepped inside and then turned around to put his arms around me. He trembled with emotion and held on to me for a few long moments before walking across his room to curl up on his bed. I gently closed the door.

I wasn't working his unit on the evening shift so I don't know how he held himself together—or perhaps fell apart—for the rest of the night. A few days later when I saw him in the hall, he shook my hand and thanked me for our talk. I never saw Brady again. I hope he's doing well.

Chapter 5   The Second Generation

"Who are you closest to?" I asked 'Hank,' who was sitting with me in the dining room at the Lakeview Youth Camp.

It was early 2002 and Hank was a resident at this open custody centre located just outside Campbell River, a fishing town about 260 kilometres north of Victoria. He was currently in Lakeview for assault. He had been in and out of Juvie for a few years but had never spent a great length of time in detention for his offences.

"Don't know. I guess I'm closest to my mom," said the seventeen-year-old whose tall, six-foot-something body loomed over mine. "I don't even see her that much, maybe twice a year."

"What about your dad?"

"Well, I guess we're friends. It's not really a father-son relationship. My parents never got married. We lived together as a family for about four years, but my dad just wanted to party all the time so my mom took me and got outta there."

As Hank grew more comfortable with our conversation, he began to share the story of his childhood.

"Just before they broke up, my dad kept on buying me things 'cause I guess he thought I'd go live with him. I did for awhile. But he had a lot of girlfriends so he didn't spend any time with me. We lived in a big house, and he used to fire up his motorbike and drive around the house showin' off. I was only seven years old and I'd have to wake up and make my own breakfast and get off to school on my own. My grandma knew what was going on at my dad's place so she gave me her number, and any time there wasn't any food, she'd come over." He stopped, and I waited patiently for him to continue.

"Then we moved and my dad didn't register me in school . . . I don't know why. We lived in this really scummy place. I wasn't even sleeping in a bed—I was sleeping on the floor. He never spent any time with me. I didn't know it then but I know now he was doing a lot of drugs. It was also at this time that I first saw him taken away by the cops."

Hank paused in his reflections. He wanted to tell me his story for the book because he thought maybe it would help some other kids facing a similar situation. The young man sipping coffee across the table from me is sincere, open and at times, quite emotional. The tape runs quiet as he ponders a hidden horror from his childhood, eyes downcast and cheeks damp with tears. Hank continued with his story, talking about his father, Andy—who I had met in the mid-seventies when I first started working in juvenile detention. My history with this family went back a long way.

"The house was full of drug dealers," Hank continued. "And everything was just right scummed out. There were two other kids, nine and ten years old. For months at a time, the parents would only see us maybe once a week and then they were gone. Us kids just did whatever we wanted so instead of goin' to school we used to go to the corner store and steal bread."

Hank's grandmother finally intervened, taking her grandson back to his mother's home where from ages nine to twelve, he lived a pretty normal life. "My mom registered me in school and things were pretty good, but I guess I had some kind of anger problems because I kept on gettin' into fights and doin' stupid s___."

Hank said that as soon as he turned twelve he began getting into more fights and running away from his mother's home. "I don't know why I did those things," he said. "It was just stupid."

His situation worsened when he returned to his dad to stay in his "crack shack." Andy was unemployed, and Hank remembered his dad and Hank's own friends waking him up in the middle of the night to show him the loot from their B&Es. There were all kinds of stolen stuff in the house, including food. Hank would just grab something to eat and go back to bed. But soon enough, Hank fell into the pot-smoking, drug-using lifestyle that was all around him. He was in serious trouble.

When Hank was thirteen, Andy went to jail for a year. Hank moved in with his grandmother and described his behaviour as going from bad to worse. The cops eventually arrested Hank and charging him with extortion and assault. The judge sentenced him to two years of probation.

Hank was not fazed. He had more brushes with the law over the next year or two before moving back with his dad. After more trouble, the courts sent Hank to the Victoria Youth Custody Centre for a series of property crimes.

While Hank was spending his youth in detention centres, his good ol' dad made sure to smuggle in weed for Hank during their visits. When he got out of Juvie he tried cocaine on his fifteenth birthday. His subsequent drug-addicted lifestyle led to further incarcerations for days or weeks at a time at Juvie in Victoria, and eventually he received a longer three-month sentence.

During our conversation, Hank said he had never been beaten up in jail although he had been hit by some of the inmates for choosing not to fight.

The last time he was in Juvie, he no longer cared about being respectful to the staff because he knew he'd be out of the youth system once he turned eighteen. His attitude back then was "I don't give a f___!" But that proved to be a bad attitude for Hank because fourteen days after he was released, the police picked him up for a robbery and he received another three month sentence at Juvie.

"Staff gave me such a hard time when I came back here because I had acted like such an idiot," Hank recalled.

I tried to encourage him to think more positively on his future. "Where do you see yourself ten years from now?"

"Hopefully in the army," he said. "I can't see myself doing anything else because I can't really see myself doing a job where I gotta wake up and show up every morning. I need a job that's kind of like jail."

Hank had learned the hard way that he needed a routine and rules to follow. I suggested he had become institutionalized, unable to draw on the self-discipline and self-motivation that most kids learn growing up.

Despite all of Hank's troublemaking, he believes he's a good person, or at least he tries to be one. "I dunno," Hank paused as he searched his memory for those things he had been taught to value, and what he had taught himself to value. "I try to treat others the way I want to be treated."

When I asked Hank how he would describe Juvie to a group of teenagers, he chuckled at first and then answered the best way he knew how. "It's the worst place in the world and you'll get the s___ kicked out of you every day, and then you sleep in scum and s___-filled cells. You get spit on. You gotta do push-ups if you swear. You get locked in your cell. That's what I'd say to 'em. That's what I tell my brothers, I want 'em to think it's the worst place ever." He added, "My dad used to tell me that Juvie was worse than adult jail, but really it's not."

"What's the best thing your dad's done for you?"

There was quite a long pause as a range of emotions crossed his face. That was a hard question, he said, repeating it quietly to himself a few times. He looked at me, and then looked down at the table.

"The best thing he did for me was go to jail last summer."

He told me certain aspects of his lifestyle began to change following Andy's last arrest and incarceration; father and son had been dealing drugs together, and all that stopped as soon as his dad was locked up in jail.

"What's the worst thing he's done to you?" I continued.

"All the lies he's told my brothers and me, and all the promises he didn't keep," he said, then quietly added, "That hurts." Hank tried to keep the tears tucked away, but he was trembling.
"I think I stopped crying about my dad when I was about eleven years old. I just gave up. I just didn't care no more . . . I have no feelings left for my dad."

He did add that he cried not long ago for his girlfriend, who is pregnant with their child. His girlfriend was the only person besides me with whom he spoke about his feelings. Hank expanded on his lack of feelings about his dad: "I still love him and all, but if he died there'd be no difference than him being alive 'cause he's just not there for me—right?"

Hank went on to say that the cops and Hank's own family would say that he had turned out to be just like Andy—just another lifer.

"But that's not the way I want to do it. In the last year or so I've just made up my mind. When I talk about this it reminds me of where I'm from and how I grew up. I like the person I am today, and if I hadn't gone through all that I wouldn't be the person I am now. I've done many wrong things but in the last year I've changed a lot—I've overcome my addictions."

As we sipped on the final dregs of our coffee, I had one last question for him. What did being tough mean to him?

"Being tough is being able to take people's s___ and just slough if off your shoulders . . . being able to go through everyday life without spazzing out, hitting something or somebody, or doing something else stupid just because you're raging."

It was an unexpected answer from a tough street kid, but perhaps his new attitude was a measure of one's ability to change despite the most difficult of family circumstances.

One afternoon, a few years before my retirement, I was sitting in the common room doing my logs (behaviour records of the residents I had supervised that shift) when I saw someone who seemed familiar. He seemed like a typical first-time admission—a tall, dark-haired fifteen-year-old wrapped in a large bathrobe, shivering like a cold dog after a night in the rain—but there was a familiarity about him.

I wondered if this boy was related to Al, a boisterous kid who was a resident back in the mid-seventies. So when the staff brought him up from admissions, I was thinking about how I would approach him. If he was Al's son and the relationship he had with his father was good, then our introduction would be easy. But—and I suspected this was more likely—if the father-son relationship wasn't so good, then I would have to be very careful about how I brought up the past.

I laid down my pen, stood up, and walked over to the boy. I said hello and asked him his name.

"Charlie," he said.

I took a deep breath.

"Was your father's name 'Al'?"

The boy looked startled. After a long pause, he asked, "Are you Gord?"

"Yes, I am," I said.

I described to Charlie how I had met his father just before I started my career at the Victoria Youth Custody Centre in 1976. I had been volunteering at the Pacific Centre for Human Development, a treatment centre for emotionally disturbed adolescents, while I was working at CFAX radio in Victoria. At the centre, I played volleyball with the kids and listened to their scheduled discussions about the six o'clock news where staff would lead talks about current affairs so that the boys would learn there was more to the world than drugs and girls! I also helped out by being available to the kids if they wanted someone to listen to them. Around this time, I met Al through my friend Bruce, a Juvie staff member working one-on-one with Al. Bruce and I would share some time working with Al and would afterwards discuss our methods of dealing with troubled kids. Sometime later, Al became a resident at the VYCC while I was working there.

After Al left the VYCC and became a father, he never forgot his time in detention. He spoke many times to his son about my and Bruce's involvement in his life, thus making Charlie's connection with me easy. As we started to talk, Charlie wanted to know what his dad was like all those years ago, but I was brief in my comments because I first wanted to hear Charlie's story.

"I hate my dad." said Charlie. "He doesn't pay any attention to me. We're not living together, and I don't see him very much."

Al's job kept him busy and on the go, so when Charlie did see his father, their time together was short on both quality and quantity. Growing up, Charlie stayed with his mom until he was thirteen and their relationship hit the rocks. He then lived in foster and group homes, becoming involved with drugs and alcohol, and causing trouble until a move onto a semi-street lifestyle led him to Juvie.

I noticed that Charlie was a quieter resident than his father had been. The boy was respectful towards me, and whenever I was working on his wing he'd ask if we could have a few minutes of conversation. Often, I would take the last hour of my shift or sometimes my own time after work to sit on the floor in the doorway of Charlie's room to chat about the day and listen to him. Our conversations covered a wide range of topics and Charlie would sometimes vent his frustrations. I always promised our conversations would be kept between us.

Over the next few years Charlie and I continued our talks in the doorway. We even kept in touch for a while after I retired and he was still in and out of Juvie.

"Do you remember my mom and dad?"

The question came from a sandy-haired sixteen-year-old as we worked together on his woodwork project. 'Daryl' had overheard my conversations with some of the other kids in wood shop that day. He had a million questions in the first thirty seconds of our introduction, and later I found out why. Daryl was adopted, and not long before we were making a mess of wood shavings on the floor, his adoptive parents had told Daryl that his birth father had been a resident years ago.

"What was my dad like when he was here?" asked Daryl as we began the first of what proved to be many conversations. He told me he was looking to meet his 'blood family.' The search had started in central British Columbia where he had been raised by his adoptive parents from the time he was a toddler. After learning that his biological father was from Victoria and had been held in the Juvie there, Daryl thought it best to move to Victoria to begin his search. His plan worked. He found both his biological mom and dad in Victoria. Unfortunately, he also found trouble and ironically ended up being an inmate, like his father before him, at the Victoria Youth Custody Centre.

"What was he like with the other kids?" asked Daryl.

I elaborated as best I could about his biological dad; after all, it was twenty-six years ago before that I had known him.

"What was he in for?" he asked.

"Don't remember," I said.

"What was he like as a resident?"

"He was High Maintenance! He was cheeky and had a lot of energy."

"Did he get into any fights?"

"Don't remember. "

"Did he talk to you much?"

"He talked as much as you're talking to me, but without so many questions," I answered.

After Daryl got out of Juvie, we met a few times to talk about his family, relationships, and his life in general. It wasn't all good times. Although he was happy that he had found his birth parents, he was deeply confused as to how to live a life with two sets of parents. This instability and insecurity consumed him, eventually sending him on a downward spiral into a dark lifestyle. Daryl was a good kid brought up by good adoptive parents, but he was letting his circumstances take him down the wrong path. The last time we met for coffee he said to me, "I won't be seeing much of you while I'm living the drug life." I haven't seen him in a number of years but the last I heard, he was in jail.

Chapter 6 In Their Own Time

Compared to Daryl, 'Kyle' seemed like he would be more likely to disappear into a lifestyle of drugs, but I've discovered in my career as a youth corrections officer that you can not predict which kids will learn from their mistakes.

Kyle liked to talk about how he was a really bad kid. Kyle was big, really rowdy, and always getting into some kind of bad stuff. He liked the adrenaline rush he got from being chased by the cops so it was a habit of his to get himself (or someone else) into trouble. Kyle said he didn't care what people thought of him.

When I asked who he was closest to, he first named a friend, but after a few minutes, said he was closest to his mother.

"She's pretty good," he said.

He said he didn't meet a kid he got along with in drug and alcohol counselling, and he especially disliked group circles.

"I don't like anyone sitting too close to me. I purposely moved my chair a little bit backwards so that there was no one behind me and I could keep an eye on everyone."

Kyle learned from an early age that he could use his size to intimidate people into keeping their distance from him, and if they got too close he would kick or punch them to keep them away. His violence towards others became a serious issue and he spent many months locked up in the VYCC, Lakeview, and Willingdon (youth detention centre in Burnaby, B.C.) for severely assaulting people. It was for assault that he found himself at Juvie again at the age of seventeen.

But this time there was something different about Kyle.

"I think I'm changing," he said. "I'm beginning to think differently about people. I've always thought that women were in a certain role and men had their own role. The man defended the woman and went out and earned money to support and look after her, but she was never an equal and couldn't work the same jobs."

"You mean you thought women should be barefoot and pregnant, and always in the kitchen?" I asked.

"No, but sort of like that. I thought women should dress like women and should be kept in their place. Now I think women are more equal—they're just as good—only different."

This new attitude changed the way he thought about his mother. He's learned to care about her and said if she ever died, he'd snap. "I would smash things. I would hurt people, probably even myself!"

About a year after our last contact inside Juvie, I saw Kyle at a car show not too far from Victoria. Kyle was a free man and a changed man. He was enjoying all of life's opportunities and was working, staying away from trouble with the law—and enjoying being a 'girl magnet.' In his body language, I sensed his respect and a little shyness.

"Everything's great," he confided. Somehow, Kyle had been able to turn his life around despite an early start in violence and time spent in Juvie.

In comparison to Kyle, 'Scott' did not end up turning his troubled life around, for reasons that were neither in nor out of his control.

Scott did not want to hand me his long-sleeved shirt in exchange for the Juvie uniform when we admitted him on an early summer day in the late seventies. When we finally got him to give his shirt to us we saw that his forearms were so heavily scarred they looked like they were covered with a fishnet. The sixteen-year-old in front of me sobbed as he tried to hide the scars.

"My mom chases my dad with a big kitchen knife yelling and swearing. Us kids don't know what to do, we're so scared. Sometimes I get so sad I use the knife on me."

After we admitted Scott, I sat with him to talk about what was happening with his family. "There are lots of fights," he said. "Yelling, swearing, hitting and throwing—my old man threw my little sister through the bedroom door. She really cried a lot after that and for a long time she'd always hide when he came home from work." Tears trickled down his cheeks as the words tumbled from his lips.

We talked for several hours over the next week or so while he was on remand to us. Scott was obviously a very distraught kid, and had some considerable difficulty relating to his peers and most adults. He was surly at times and wanted to be left alone. He spent a lot of time in East #1, an observation cell that was close to both the common area (the television room) and to staff. We kept a close eye on him, watching for any possibilities of the boy harming himself or someone else.

Scott managed to find a way to harm himself. While he was in East #1, staff caught him smashing his head against the concrete wall. Blood from his forehead was smeared on the wall over the steel bunk and smudged the window on the door as well as the window that looked outside. Scott was frenzied, swearing and pacing and wiping his bloodied hands all over himself and everything he touched. We talked to the boy quietly and were able to get him to move willingly to the time-out room where staff supervised him while he cleaned himself up. Afterwards, a staff member observed him while he cleaned up the mess he had made.

I accompanied a probation officer to Scott's home to inform

the boy and his family that the Ministry was considering an 'apprehension,' which meant that government authorities would legally remove Scott from his family. The Ministry would then place Scott in 'special therapeutic care'—a foster home or group home.

About twenty-five minutes after the probation officer entered the house, she came out of the place in tears. She said the family ganged up on her, denying that there were any problems! They accused her of interfering and being the reason that their son was so upset, and then they insulted and ridiculed her until she left. Scott sided with his family through this whole episode.

Shortly after this happened Scott killed himself. Most of the staff members at the VYCC were shocked, but not surprised, that this desperate and tortured boy had taken his own life.

RAW VOICES III

Poem: "The Eye of the Beholder"

A second poem from a resident in the mid-eighties:

. . . Old and wrinkled,
Soft and sprinkled
Can have a smile that warms
the heart.

Both to me
Are beauty to see
If the smile plays it's merry
part.

Does all turn grey
And fade away
When in our world, it gets
older?

Of what we see
The true beauty be
In the eye of the beholder.

Chapter 7   Open Custody

How do I feel about things? I think everything sucks. Never once in my life have I been truly happy. I've always looked at my friends and seen how they lived and thought, damn I wish I was in their shoes . . . . You know what? The closer I get to going to court, the longer I feel I'm going to be here for.

'Gerry' wrote me this letter from Lakeview Youth Camp while waiting to go to court. It was the late eighties and Gerry was sixteen and had been in and out of Juvie several times. Lakeview was nestled in densely-forested mountains about four kilometres off the Vancouver Island Highway, forty kilometres north of Campbell River. Originally a logging camp, the site was first used in the mid-seventies as an open custody youth centre. It evolved from an army barracks style of dorm complex with a camp kitchen to a multiplex of administration, program, recreation and living units for approximately thirty males. Lakeview had programs for school, arts and crafts, and woodworking. It had an outdoor basketball court, an indoor gym, an Alaskan saw mill, and the lake of course. Residents were responsible for the ongoing beautification and basic upkeep of the site, which was great for focusing and taming those teenaged boys' high energy!

I'm scared Gord, I can't stand being around so many people who would rather hurt me than be my friend. I hate the fact that you have to be a hardcore criminal to have friends in here, otherwise you're just a geek. People who know me don't believe that I want to turn my life around, but if they compared my behaviour from now to my behaviour the first time in Juvie, I think they would believe me a lot more. Right now I feel like a little kid, because all I want is my mommy. If my mom was here I would hug her forever.

I don't belong with all these criminals. Just because I've done a little bit of crime that doesn't mean I'm a criminal, does it? I wish the judge today would realize I don't belong here and release me. Do you think I belong here? I think I need help, and a lot of it, but I wouldn't call this "help," if anything it might be shock therapy but that isn't going to help me. You know what, every time I got out of here I said to myself I'm not coming back and this time I mean it more than I've ever meant anything. The thing is it's hard to prove yourself when you're rotting in a jail cell. The first time I was in here I meant it when I said I wasn't coming back, and I did pretty good, it took me two years to come back for something that wasn't a breach of my probation order. I think that's pretty good, better than most people, but I guess it wasn't quite good enough. I wish they'd hurry up and send me to court, the suspense is killing me.

When I first talked to my mom I just burst into tears, it felt so good to hear her voice again, I can't wait to see her again, hopefully I'll get out today so I can see her today. I wonder if my mom hurts as much as I do, she probably hurts more actually. Right now I wish I could start my whole life over again, it's not fair that I have to live like this. I've never purposely harmed anyone in my life, except for the kids I robbed, but I'm so remorseful for that, I can't even begin to explain how much. Why did I ruin my life like this? If I had a knife right now, I would be dead, and all the pain would end with me. I don't want to live like this Gord. I just wish I had realized this two years ago. I know one day I'll probably look back at this and laugh, but right now all I can do is look ahead and cry. Why is it that when I ask God for help it almost never gets answered?

Previous to this letter, Gerry had received a court order to complete part of his probation in a wilderness survival program called Coastline Challenges, a physical regime of climbing, rappelling, running, swimming, and group therapy aimed at teaching personal accountability and responsibility. It had been his second try at Coastline. The first time he was there he had skipped his graduation, so he was sent back to Lakeview for two weeks. After Lakeview, he returned to Coastline Challenges for another try at completing the program.

Gerry did make it the whole way through the second time and was proud to have finally graduated. He said he actually enjoyed the program quite a bit. He still had five more months of his probation left so he signed up to be a volunteer at Coastline and he said he was excited to be moving in with his mom when his probation wrapped up. Gerry was happy to have found the focus and responsibility Coastline Challenges gave him—and to have the hiking gear, backpack, and sleeping bag they gave him for attending the annual services meeting!

But as life goes, sometimes things don't work out the way you want them to. For some reason Gerry's volunteer job at Coastlines fell through and he got into more trouble with the law and the courts told him to go back to Lakeview for his remand. From Lakeview, Gerry wrote me another letter and explained his situation.

My remaining charges are mischief (guilty), assault x 2 (kind of guilty and kind of not guilty), and assault on an officer (definitely not guilty).

Gerry said that when he arrived at Lakeview this time it was not as bad as he had expected. He said he wasn't making friends quickly, but he didn't have any real problems. He had to spend Christmas there, which he hated. On Christmas Day the kids each got a couple of pens, a toothbrush, a book, an Archie comic, a notebook and a game. Gerry said the meals were really good and they watched a great movie but other than that, Christmas Day was long and boring. He also told me about his behaviour at the camp. Every day, the staff would record the residents' behaviour and attitude on a scale from one (bad) to five (very good).

I am pretty much on level three but when I got here I started on level two. I have begun working out four times a week, which helped quite a bit with my score. While I am here I am going to be getting involved in drug and alcohol counselling, anti-offending counselling, and school. With all that how can I even stand a chance of screwing up again?

Gerry continued with his typical frankness.

You know what, this place is actually a lot better than VYCC, and I'm kind of glad I'm here, but I miss my mom and I miss you. I'm trying to make a lot of positive changes, and I'm glad of that. I really miss being with my friends and the people I love. Some people who come to jail make lots of friends and enjoy themselves. I find that hard to do. I don't want to be friends with most of the people in here. Since I have been in custody I have wished I was dead quite a few times. It's hard for me to be like this. I'm used to being friends with everyone I meet except for in jail I guess.

After that last letter, Gerry went to court to face his charges and then serve his sentence. Later he got a job in Victoria, moving on from the youth detention system to completely supporting himself as an independent young man.

I met 'Barry' during his nearly one year remand at the Victoria Youth Custody Centre. He was a gifted boy who had skipped a couple of grades in school. He wasn't shy in letting you know how smart he was with a quiet smile. When he finally faced the court to receive his sentence, the judge sent him to Lakeview. Shortly after his arrival Barry sent me this letter:

Gord, I'm doing fine. It's my second day here in Lakeview, and I'm still in shock. This place is so different. I'm in my own room. It's a room, not a cell. I have two windows. One of them opens. My floor is carpeted. I have my own desk and closet. I can open my door anytime I want. I can go outside. I spent the last two days just sitting outside on the grass. Even the rain was spectacular. We overlook a lake with a mountain directly behind it. I haven't seen the top of it because it disappears into the clouds. There is snow on it that stays there until May. I've had one can of Coke since I came in. It was memorable. I'm in a large cabin with five guys. They are all bent on not re-offending so it's the perfect atmosphere for me. They are all nice towards me. This isn't a jail. It's a place for teens who want to change their lives around. I'm fitting in fairly well. Although my sentence here is for a long time, seven months, I could do it here way easier than at VYCC. I have to say the staff here is fairly relaxed. I could have AWOL'd so many times. They trust us. It's great. Anyone who AWOLs from here is dumb. The main concern here is anti-offending, and if you leave, you obviously want to re-offend. I want to talk to you. I could probably get you on my phone list. I don't know, what do you think? Now the thing I miss most is my dog. Hey, soon I can get temporary absences, some up to five days long. I could go home! Or fly to Mexico and back. A lot can be done in five days. This place opens doors. Write back soon.

He did his time and got out, determined not to re-offend. There isn't an easy way to say what happened next. Barry died in an accident after his time at Lakeview. It was with some anxiety and nervousness that I went to visit Barry's parents. I wanted to share his letters with them, and to give them a photograph of Barry and me at Lakeview. His parents warmly welcomed me into their home. I showed them the list of things he wanted to do with his life: climb Mount Everest, scuba dive, write a book, and have children.

Unfortunately, the British Columbia Government closed Lakeview Youth Camp in the autumn of 2003. Today, most kids who would have been sentenced to stay at Lakeview are now housed in the maximum-security Victoria Youth Custody Centre where two of the four units are designated as "open custody" within the confines of the closed custody centre.

At my request, Barry's father shares his insights:

The initial impression most of us have when thinking about juvenile detention is a negative one and usually for good reason. It's disturbing to think of our youth misbehaving to the point that they need to be locked up, either as a potential rehabilitation tool or worse, to protect the rest of society from their escalating criminal activities. I must confess I hadn't given it a lot of thought until one of our children took a turn down the wrong road.

We had been prepared to a certain degree for the unexpected by our eldest. He began to change at about the age of 14—grade nine. The desire to be accepted by the "cool" group of peers pushed him away from his parents and encouraged rebellious and assertive behavior. The peak for this difficult time came when he was about 16. Fortunately, it gradually improved as he matured. I'm sure most parents of teenagers can well relate to this difficult phase. Our next son, two years younger, became influenced in the same way at about the same age—grade nine. However, he moved from his childhood circle of friends to a new more rambunctious group. He considered them to be "cool" and he wanted to be accepted.

I'm not sure which came first, the drugs or the petty crime. Whichever it was they soon became intertwined and inseparable. As a parent, you want to believe your children when they tell you what they are and what they aren't up to. Unfortunately, chronic and sometimes pathological lying comes with the drugs and criminal behavior. It started with pot smoking and theft from cars. Although the drugs didn't escalate much past pot, maybe some mild chemicals, the usage increased to every day. The break, enter and thefts also increased. We found stolen property in our house. We confronted him and asked for honest answers. We didn't get them. All we got was his rage. We made a decision to call the police. We felt we had to do something and that seemed to be the only option we had. We had now entered the youth justice system.

Despite our attempts to stop things cold by getting the authorities involved, things escalated. We even moved way across town in our attempts to limit the involvement with the friends. Of course we were never completely in the know but we strongly suspected things hadn't really changed. That suspicion turned to reality when the police came to arrest him for a very serious crime. We entered the system again, this time however, there would be no warnings, it was time to send a message.

We got to see first hand how the legal system for juveniles works. There was nothing pleasant about the experience but what I can say is I was generally impressed with the quality of people we have working in it. We had caring and competent defense attorneys appointed for him by the court. They were overworked but did a credible job nonetheless. The court officials were for the most part courteous and respectful. During those couple of years there were a number of police officers that had been involved in the cases. The majority appeared to have some concern and compassion for the kids, particularly if they felt some learning from the mistakes was possible. We did experience a few overzealous, humourless cops as well. I guess that goes with the territory.

The other officers of the court who made an impression were the judges. They were respectful to the kids at all times and made a genuine effort to impose the right sentence. All arguments and positions were considered before a reasoned comment was delivered. I guess that's why we have them there doing that job but, nonetheless, they made a difficult job look easy.

Our son experienced two detention centres, the old facility in Victoria and Lakeview in Campbell River. It sounded like there were some pretty messed up kids in Victoria. A number were violent and a number were regular guests. The worry for us, and probably the corrections officials, was that weaker kids could become victimized and vulnerable ones could learn more criminal techniques—a crime school of sorts. Fortunately, being a bright kid, he sized up the inmates and guards quickly. He knew which kids to stay away from and what behaviours would get rewarded by the guards. He ended up in the most desirable section within a week or two. His good behaviour earned him the opportunity to transfer to Lakeview—an open style facility.

During our visits with him it became clear that he knew he had done wrong and it was time to straighten out. He had the good fortune to get to know a number of the guards and counsellors during his time there. They generally took the time to help the ones who were ready to change directions in their lives. I believe the flexibility that can be built in to this rigid system is very important.

What I mean by this is most of the kids in the detention system are probably salvageable; rehabilitation will succeed. In order for this to happen we have to recognize that they all have different buttons that need to be pushed. We have to make sure that there is enough flexibility within the detention framework to allow and encourage growth. After all, these are young, unfinished projects. Most are between 15 and 18 years of age. Those years can be the most difficult ones to go through in anyone's life. What can be an unruly, miserable teenager at 16 can be a productive, sensitive adult at 22. We can't lose sight of that.

What we also can't lose sight of is the fact that some of these young offenders are just bad apples. Maybe we can't rehabilitate them all. We can certainly try but for those ones the important issue is to protect society — keep them off the streets for a while. In addition it's probably important to keep them somewhat segregated from other inmates who are less likely to re-offend. As mentioned earlier, we don't want the hardened ones passing a criminal education on to the novices in the system. Certain types of segregation could keep the vulnerable ones from re-connecting with the bad ones after release as well. The lack of opportunity to form relationships while inside could be enough to discourage it on the outside.

No family's experience with juvie will be a happy one but for most it could be a positive one. If our kids can learn from their mistakes and Juvie helps in that process then it is serving a valuable function. Our son learned from his experience in detention — he didn't become perfect but he learned, grew and became a big part of our family again and that's all we could ask for.

On a closing note, I think it is important for society to understand that everyone has a role in the safe development of our youth. There is a tendency to point the finger at the parents and label them as "bad". In many cases this may be justified. Homes broken by infidelity and anger, alcohol and drug abuse can certainly lead to little or no parenting within the home. These kids end up modeling on the negative behaviours they see at home and on the street with their chosen peers.

However, I believe there are a large number of kids out there that are "experimenting with crime just as they are experimenting with drugs and alcohol. They come from homes that we would identify as good homes with "good" parents. Most of them get through the teen years without going too far or without getting caught. Just because yours doesn't get caught doesn't mean it's not happening.

All of us, including those without children, have to recognize that we play a role in growing our youth. The easiest way to keep kids from drugs and crime is to keep them busy doing things that they enjoy. Less spare time means less time available for harmful activities. Of course there is a balance and kids do need their own time to play and hang out with friends. Our job is to keep the balance possible by providing community sports programs and facilities; arts, music and dance programs in our communities and schools; boys and girls clubs etc. The list does go on but the key point is if we don't want our young to be locked away during the important development years, all of society has to continue to invest time and money to help guide and sometimes push them down the right paths.

Barry's Father
Victoria 2006

Chapter 8   A Personal Adventure with Fostering

In the early 1980s, the provincial government placed Ray, an eleven-year-old, with me as a special-care foster child. The placement was a good match. He stayed with me for ten years, leaving only to get married! For a foster child to live with his sponsor family that length of time is unusual since many foster home matches average less than a year and then the young person moves on for either good or bad reasons. Ray's single admission to Juvie when he was fourteen was the only time he spent in Juvie. During his teenage years, he was involved in other 'troublemaking' incidents, but they were of a minor nature and were dealt with by his social worker and myself.

Ray's life before I met him was, to say the least, horrendous. Before coming to stay with me, his family life was inconsistent and disruptive. At six, he was buying milk and bananas with money from the sale of empty beer cans and pop bottles because there was no food in the house. Ray's 'grocery shopping' had to feed him and two other siblings. According to Ray, the placement with me was the beginning of the most stable part of his life. As a foster child in my home, he did all the normal things kids did at his age—he palled around with friends, played sports, and enjoyed our holiday trips. His teen years were relatively trouble free, except when he was fourteen and had that brief overnight stay at Juvie, followed by community hours and probation.

At twenty-one, he moved out to be married. Unfortunately, all the turmoil from his young life started to manifest at this time and Ray developed a serious drinking problem early on as a new husband. Four years and two sons later, the marriage dissolved. Despite his alcoholism, he maintained steady employment throughout his twenties and beyond. His employers labeled him an excellent worker, reliable and proficient, and a good organizer possessing a magnetic personality. A few years after the divorce, Ray was not visiting his kids on any kind of a regular basis. With his permission, I share Ray's battle with alcoholism over the years. He has written to me from detox centres and rehab houses around British Columbia. His letters are from the heart, expressive of the pain, remorse, and confusion of his dysfunctional family life from infancy to ten years old, followed by "this f___ing monster, alcoholism!" in his adult years.

From spring 1999:

Since November I've been in jail again: detox. I just got my thirty-day tag from A.A. and N.A. Did you see the boys over the holidays? I got really f___ed up this time. I am sick of being this way. I was in the hospital in the beginning of February for a week. I died. They had to monitor my heart. It really sucks being alone with no support or anyone to talk to about stuff and lonely. I spent Christmas at the Mustard Seed with street friends, good f___in' life eh! I have to stop hurting myself and others around me without even noticing or caring. This disease is powerful man and I don't want to die a druggie or a drunk. Have the boys stopped asking about me?

And this letter, later that same year:

I sit here wondering if I should leave or stay, sometimes it just gets very confusing. I get so frustrated it's unbearable. But the outcome is I'm still here. But things are still going according to plan. I got some job offers but I'm just not ready to do anything like that yet. I am really serious this time I know I've said it before but after almost dying it is scary. I've got an email account at the library it's so cool I sit there for hours. Hey Gord, how about some pictures of the boys please, I miss them.

Early summer 1999:

Well I've been in recovery several months now. I am learning a lot of values of life here and trying to build up my self-confidence and pride again. It's a hard long process but I am coming along. I feel as if I am doing to my family as what my dad did to us. I feel really s__ty about everything that's going on. . . . I've lost everything that I've worked hard to build up, and it really hurts me. Sometimes I just want to freak right out but it won't prove nothing if I do.

Ray told me that while at the recovery centre he'd met a nurse addicted to booze and cocaine, a professor addicted to heroin, and a woman from the provincial government addicted to Valium and cocaine. People as young as nineteen and as old as seventy-five were there for treatment. They were street bums, drug dealers, working class guys, and all the way up the social ladder to high-flying professionals.

Well another birthday and no contact because of my stupidity! (It was his oldest boy's birthday. Ray's ex-wife had obtained full custody of the boys because of the alcoholism so he had no contact with his sons.) *Oh well when the time is right and if the kids want to see me I'll be there. And if not that will just be something I have to deal with—I am going through a healing process with myself and it's scary. To deal with things and really actually wanting to do it this time and not getting forced or told to is really weird. Issues arise and can hurt and be emotional but dealing with it at a different state sure is weird. The process takes a long frustrating time . . . pataince is a virtue I can't even spell!!*

After this letter, Ray left the recovery house to work part-time:

Man, Gord, was it ever tough not to drink because everywhere I went there was a beer store. I must have walked by a liquor store about ten times, but I just went to the SuperValu and came home. I am really proud of myself. All the old feelings came back, it was really weird and scary. When you come up again we'll go for coffee or if you're lucky I'll cook supper.

I think people abuse themselves because they try to forget their problems or just plain don't want to deal with them. Sure it takes your mind away from everything until you wake up, if you sleep, then you do it all over again and again. What people don't realize is that how many people, friends and loved ones, you hurt until it's too late. And when it's too late no one is there for you. Only until you yourself have to commit to recovery, then you will notice that people are there behind you. But they don't particularly come out and say, "You need help," it only comes when you really want to do it from the heart and the brain.

As Ray continues to struggle today with his health and his place in the world, I wanted to pass on some of Ray's words of advice for people who think they may be dealing with drug or alcohol abusers:

- Your first suspicion of their addictions probably occurs a year

after they've begun abusing drugs and alcohol
- Their remorse for their addictions may be false
- Don't do everything for them. They need to deal with their recovery themselves. The best thing you can do support them by being there and listening
- Rehab is thirty days of just drying out, but the length of stay is an individual choice
- Some may have to go to rehab more than one time
- Work hard to improve the quality of your relationship with family members
- Addiction is a lifelong struggle
- There is hope

▲ Old centre, Pembroke St. Victoria passageway to youth court

▼ Victoria Youth Custody Centre, staff escort residents to living unit

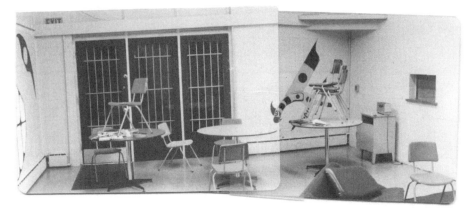

▲ Victoria Youth Custody east (boys) wing, mid-seventies

◄ Victoria Youth Custody recreation courtyard, mid-seventies

◄ Victoria Youth Custody east (boys) wing, mid-seventies

◄ Victoria Youth Custody Centre, boys wing, present-day

◄ Victoria Youth Custody Centre recreation area and living unit, present day

◄ Victoria Youth Custody double room new centre, present day

◄ Victoria Youth Custody Centre, two-level living unit, present day

◄ Lakeview Open Custody near Campbell River on Vancouver Island; youth housing on right

PART TWO

Adults & Teenagers:
Relationships in Crisis

Chapter 9 A Career Working with Troubled Youth

Handcuffed to my wrist, he stood quietly over the open casket with no tears, no expression and no words. We stood in heavy silence for about a minute, and then not able to voice a feeling, he tugged at the cuffs and we moved away. It was a sixteen-year-old boy's last look at his mother.

The tumultuous family life of many of our residents sometimes involves the death of a parent or sibling. If the death occurs while a juvenile is in custody, the centre will often grant a special temporary absence (TA) so he or she can attend the funeral. In this particular case, I had come to know the boy fairly well over his several admissions into the VYCC, and he asked if I would take him on a TA to the viewing and the funeral.

A street church hosted the respectful afternoon ceremony for his late mother. The boy was a pallbearer, so it was a little awkward since he had to remain handcuffed to me the whole time. However, things went smoothly and he introduced my fellow staff and me to his family and siblings who thanked us for bringing him to the funeral.

The boy's mother had visited him at the custody centre two days prior to her death. He said the visit had gone well with good conversation, but his mom was high on something, maybe cocaine, and he said he had a feeling that he might not see her again. As if all this was not enough, several months before his mother's early death, his step-dad had committed suicide—the boy himself discovered the man's body in a closet. The tragedies of this sixteen-year-old's life were more than most of us bear in a lifetime.

The custody centre staff has the choice to say yes or no when these TAs to funerals come up. Some say no; it's a very difficult and emotional decision to escort a kid into a public and often very personal event. I have done two other TA funeral escorts without incident, but this was the only one with handcuffs. And for myself, I appreciated that I did not have to wear the corrections uniform that would have made the boy stand out from the crowd. How embarrassing that would have been for the kid on top of being cuffed to someone.

Attendance at a funeral as a resident's escort does not occur often but difficult emotional situations are part of the job, along with dealing with attempted suicides, extreme violence and psychotic episodes. Despite all these stresses, I have learned that working with kids is a privilege. Watching their lives crumble beyond repair and then seeing some of these kids put themselves back together bit by bit, and being able to provide a safe environment for them to share their emotions with during these rough times are rewards that my coworkers and I must handle with responsibility and care.

Why work with kids? The reasons are as varied as the kinds of people who work in the jails and custody centres: money, compassion, tributes, paid and extended holidays, power or prestige. We can get some, none, all of the above or more than what we expected on the job.

In the open and closed institutions in this country there are security officers, correctional officers, youth supervisors, line staff, program staff, teaching staff, shift supervisors, directors of programming, managers of operations, directors of institutions and regional managers. Sometimes Juvie is a stepping stone for the ambitious. It's common for some staff members to start in Juvie before seeking a good job outside of the centre through a secondment, which can be a great stress reliever. A secondment refers to filling in at another job in another part of government on a temporary basis with the potential of getting a permanent job out of the placement.

Outside of the institutional setting, there are more ways to work with young offenders. Through my work inside Juvie, I've met childcare counsellors, psychiatric nurses, social workers, alternative school teachers, probation officers, foster parents and group home workers who care for and work with the kids once they get out of custody. And through a group of volunteers, I also met a very nice lady to whom I am still attached!

Stress is very real. Stress—mental or physical tension or force that strains or deforms—dictionary definitions of an illness that wasn't even recognized in the mid-70's. One can't reach inside and pull out the stress like a nail you've stepped on, but this emotional pus will seek a draining one way or another, and the draining is the side we do see.

These career paths can create many levels of mental, emotional, and physical stress that can cause workers to unleash their frustrations on family, co-workers and residents. The stress can even cause staff to steal from fellow co-workers and residents—I've seen it happen. There's no denying that the youth corrections setting can be a negative environment. It is emotionally challenging and draining. Sudden unpredictable acts of violence constantly threaten any periods of peace. If you are a parent, think of the worst times you had with your teenager. Now place your child among fifteen other teenagers that are also short-fused and ready to blow in a confined, institutional space—that's what it's like to work in a youth custody centre. It is your job to keep the lid on this seething cauldron of hormones!

Experience is proof of usefulness. Many staff are not aware of why they want to work with kids. A coping strategy is a necessary part of the bagful of skills which you take to work. Balance, common sense, experience, insight and understanding through knowledge are the cornerstones of coping and harvesting a long and satisfying career with kids.

It's necessary when training new staff to know why they work with kids, know what the need they wish to satisfy is. Here are some suggestions gleaned from staff:

- Control.
- Power to have the authority to punish.
- "I want to save the kids."
- "I know what's best for them."
- "I like working with kids."
- "I have ability with kids."
- "Kids listen to me."
- "I don't have any kids of my own. "
- "I understand kids."
- "I have skills and knowledge."
- "I'm a good listener; kids are interesting."
- The money and time off are really good.
- "I think I would like to broaden my experience in government."
- "I like sports; I think I can offer a lot."

If you want to work with troubled kids and understand enough about yourself to know why, you're a good deal along the way to being able to cope with the stress of the job. Understanding your work and balancing the negative with some sort of positive is very necessary. My girlfriends and family over the years were a great outlet for me. Friends not even in the kid business many times offered insightful comments that increased my understanding — some of these were my old broadcast friends.

"That staffer never took his eyes off of the kids all the time we were here," Boyd Kozak commented on his tour of the centre. Renowned as an enthusiastic, extroverted and professional Winnipeg broadcaster, Boyd was quite subdued as we left the centre. Later outside, he commented, "That is a very difficult job."

As a staff member, I had to consider government philosophies, policies and procedures, the Police Act, the Corrections Act, the Young Offenders Act, the Juvenile Delinquents Act, the Youth Criminal Justice Act and union and management issues that seemed to be always in a state of revision. Plus, everybody has their own opinion about what we should do with the kids. In my experience, I never wanted to let down my fellow staff members, so I was always putting pressure on myself to support them. And of course the kids expected you to follow their demands. Having to deal with all this when your emotional batteries are low can lead very quickly to burnout. I have learned that having a coping strategy that involves staying physically healthy and having a support system made up of a spouse, family and friends are as essential as the bagful of skills you need to take to work.

Being able to get along with most of the kids definitely makes the job easier. It's an asset to be approachable to the residents because it makes it easier to enforce the rules, which is a necessary part of the job. When it came time to set down the rules, I tried to be as firm and fair with the kids as possible and I believe it worked.

"Twenty-five!" was the staff directive to the kids when they swore. Twenty-five push-ups for every swear word wasn't demeaning but the kid would definitely feel the consequences.

Swearing stayed at a minimum at our centre. Sometimes I would allow a curse or two to go by without calling them on it because so many of these kids are from the street where swearing is part of their language and half the time they don't even realize they are swearing. And because of that understanding, they respected that I acknowledged where they came from.

If residents were caught smoking they had to be in their cell for three hours while all their friends enjoyed free time. For the most part, our disciplinary actions for breaking the rules were successful and we managed to keep a reasonable control on the residents' behaviour.

If staff members are not enthusiastic about working with the kids, their careers will be less than interesting. We all start (or, most of us start) with an attitude of wanting to help the kids, and as we journey through our working years we learn how best to do this. And of course we always tend to think our way is better. Sticking to one's own way is acceptable if you're making coffee or cooking a steak, but when you're working with kids the challenge is to be able to work effectively as part of a team of professionals to supervise a group of upset youngsters who all want to behave in their own way.

Being at the VYCC for over twenty-six years, it was unique for me to see ex-residents become staff at the centre. Two men who were residents when I first started at Juvie showed up years later as line staff that I actually worked side-by-side with on the East Wing. These men were very good at supervising the residents because they were firm, fair and fun. They influenced me to develop greater patience and tolerance, and helped me improve my understanding of troubled kids. It took most staff members many years to learn what these two men had already internalized as residents years before—their first day on the job was old history!

When I worked with these guys they would say, "I remember acting like that—was I really that stupid?" Or, "I can see how and why I ended up here." And often, "How did my mom ever put up with me?"

The shock of finding oneself in a serious altercation with a kid can be very upsetting to the "new fish"—the label given new staff members by the residents. The "new fish" would often question their own abilities to cope with the kids and say, "They never told us about this kind of s___ at the JI!" (The Justice Institute in the Lower Mainland is where most staff members are trained.)

People can prepare for work in a youth custody centre in a variety of ways. In British Columbia, most of the men and women hired today have much more than the basic Grade 12 education. College certificates and university degrees in the social sciences, criminology, and psychology help staff to understand the client and the system and ongoing training and upgrading is available for all corrections staff. During the time I was working, staff members had access to approximately ten days of courses or training every three years. Workshops and programs included courses on the mentally disordered young offender, the adolescent sex offender, the female young offender, group supervising and conflict resolution, among many others.

As I mentioned in the introduction to this book, when I started my career working with troubled youth during the seventies I came from a roundabout route. In 1976, I was thirty-four and had been a foster parent for three years when I began working at the Victoria Youth Custody Centre. In addition to the foster parenting, I had been a probation sponsor with Family Court in Victoria and as a Big Brother, I was among five men and women who founded the Victoria chapter of Big Brothers in the late sixties.

A number of men and women who work at youth custody centres also came from diverse career paths. Mature individuals with an understanding of the rough and tumble 'school of hard knocks' often become capable, reliable and effective staff members. Personally, I would like to see a good balance of older men and women—aged forty to sixty, for example—working with kids as they would provide a steadying influence over some very unsteady young personalities.

Of course, not everyone is suited to working with these kids. One midnight shift in midsummer, the Victoria Police called to tell us that a drunken fifteen-year-old was on his way. A social worker, transferred from a small town in Eastern British Columbia, had just joined us as our newest staff member and was keen to deal with this troubled, "Big City" kid. The social worker helped us hold the kid up in the shower. The boy's cut-offs were soaked with wine puke so we cleaned him up and parked him in the time-out cell until his sobriety set in. His reeking hangover must have taught him a good lesson because we never saw the boy again, along with the social worker who quit the very next day.

Being part of a young person's life is a privilege. Whether we barely touch the surface of their lives or become a life-altering mentor, our actions must be motivated by the very best intentions. We must always be respectful and remember that beneath these kids' tough exteriors, there may be goodness.

RAW VOICES IV

Letter: "Marty"

Marty was writing me from Toronto in the early eighties. He was bringing me up to date after a few years of not hearing from him.

I'm thinking of going back to school . . . I have appointments for enrollment tomorrow.

I've learned to love Toronto . . . I've met a lot of people here . . . I was doing stage work with bands . . . I have a girlfriend.

My mom and sister moved back to Victoria. We don't seem to communicate with each other much. I got a birthday card from my sister and one depressing letter from my mom in almost two years. My mother has diabetes and my sister's been shoplifting. F___ I hope she doesn't do what I did I will "kill" her. If [my sister] turns up in Juvie give me a letter so I can write her and try and talk some sense in to her. That was my problem. If it was not for you, Gord, I would have probably wound up like poor ["David", from Chapter 2], or one of the many other kids who really never had anyone who gave a s___.

Please write back I miss your friendship.

Chapter 10   Listening

The most frequent comment I heard when helping kids through their tough times was, "You don't need to fix it, just listen to me!" I have learned that listening—without judgment!—and developing an atmosphere of trust and honesty provides a nurturing space for a young person to grow emotionally and deepen self-awareness. They need a safe environment where they feel they can be heard and they require empathic feedback in order to begin to untangle years of emotional confusion.

In my twenty-six-year career working in youth custody I've learned the value of good listening skills. The best questions come from an intelligent response to what you hear the person saying. In other words, if you're trying to word your next interview question in your mind while the kid is speaking, then you're not really listening. How often do we wait for the other person to finish talking so we can jump in with what we feel we absolutely must say? When I think of the reason why I enjoy a particular person's company, it is often because he or she listens attentively to what I'm saying. It feels good to be listened to: you feel recognized, that your opinion matters and that your words are important. Every person needs this and young people especially thrive on being heard and accepted.

Listening is an art. Listening assumes a self-assurance that does not need constant reaffirmation. If you know yourself it means that you are able to set aside your own needs while focusing on another's. Hearing the voice is the mechanical part but understanding the speaker, asking questions and giving feedback at the appropriate time is the creative part of communication. Trust and confidentiality are important elements in ensuring a safe place for your friend or child to speak—and continue to want to speak to you again.

I've also learned that kids form an opinion of you based on your actions, so following through with what you said you would do earns you credibility. The residents at Juvie would watch how the staff treated other residents and would spot those who carried an agenda—agendas that could be used by the kids against the staff at a later date. Therefore, approaching each situation with respect and just being yourself was the key to keeping the peace and to teaching the residents some values.

"We don't always have to talk about my problems," said a sixteen-year-old when we were getting together for another coffee one day. His comment taught me that balance is important; having time for both fun and seriousness is what improves the quality and depth of friendship.

If I could sum up, my most important role in my years working with teenagers was to listen. This statement is on a picture that hangs in the entrance of the Victoria Youth Custody Centre.

Chapter 11　Parenting

"The child is father to the man."

As parents, we have a profound responsibility when we prepare a child for their life's journey. There are no guarantees of course but a basic "I just want to be normal" upbringing is a good place to start.

The powerful message of Hank's story was one of the reasons I wrote this book because children learn what they live, and then live what they have seen. Many questions came to mind when I wrote his story. Where were social services? Why was his grandma not given more support? Wasn't the landlord aware of what his renters were doing? Who checks up on kids when they aren't in school? What were the courts and the police doing to keep this boy safe? Early intervention, family support, and follow-through from social services would certainly have been appropriate for this young boy, but for a myriad of reasons—actually excuses, I think—nothing happened for two generations in Hank's family.

Hank's story is similar to those of many Juvie kids and yet not like many others. It's wrong to tar all young offenders with the same brush because each of their stories will be different. Children can screw up or succeed whether they're rich or poor or from two-parent, single-parent or no-parent situations. Psychological disorders, learning disabilities, abuse, neglect, and peer pressure can affect a child's life entirely, partially, or barely at all, and that's why I think society has a responsibility to do its best to prepare and support kids, regardless of their life situation.

In a quiet and lengthy conversation, a seventeen-year-old

convicted of murder shared with me some of his feelings about his family: "I told the social workers that my mom wasn't responsible enough to look after us kids but they didn't do anything. That was when I was thirteen, now look what's happened." Now he's in jail for murder.

Perhaps his crime could have been prevented but I don't know that. I do know that social workers are stretched to their limits, only having so much time for each client, and sometimes families reject their efforts to help.

From a fifteen-year-old boy in a British Columbia youth correctional program: "Well it was a drag watching you drive away yesterday. I had tears running down my face and I tried to hold them back but I couldn't, it really hurt inside of me when you said goodbye, it sounded like you were saying goodbye for ever, but I know you wouldn't do that to me . . . .. There is something inside me when I see you or talk to you that makes me feel really good so if I have any problems when I get out of here, do you mind if I phone you so I could talk to you for a while because you're the only one I really can talk to."

That tearful boy watching me leave had not one caring connection with an adult and had to seek that contact outside of his family, from a youth supervisor in a jail! Parents have a responsibility to provide this closeness and safety for their kids to speak. Each kid has something honest, profound, blunt, open, scary, significant, poignant and revealing to say to you if you give them the time and opportunity to open up. A thousand books couldn't contain the stories and revelations of troubled kids that youth-supervising staff members are exposed to in their career.

The long-term, two-generation friendships that I have had with Charlie and his father Al, along with several other families, have disturbed me. I am sad for these young men and women and the emotional turmoil they have passed down to their own children. I don't like to see Juvie as a revolving door in the lives of these troubled families. What are the answers? I don't know, and I think no one really knows. There is no secret formula that will solve these kids' and their families' problems and make everyone better, but I do know that children and teenagers crave connection that is appropriate, consistent and loving. We have to nip their antisocial behaviours in the bud by showing them by example, values of respect, accountability and the satisfaction of hard work.

So many kids have said to me, "I just want to be normal!" My response to them was, "What do you mean by normal?"

To many, normal meant a mom, dad, family, friends and school. So what were these so-called bad kids saying to me? Surprisingly, good normal things. They wanted their mom and dad to be there for them. Even if they were divorced and living apart, the kids wanted to feel like their parents were making an effort to remain involved in their lives. Supportive and conscientious family relationships provide a foundation for children to confidently strike up friendships with kids their own age and to act respectfully in the community; and strong families often prevent youth from getting into serious trouble with the law.

I think adults who work with young people must have an understanding—first of themselves and then of children, knowing that growing up is a series of learning steps. One of the ways kids learn is by making mistakes, and showing them why something was a mistake and how to correct it is a traditional teaching role of parents. But when parents are not performing these common tasks, either the kid learns or doesn't learn from his or her own mistakes.

If they're lucky, someone in the community will step up to teach them. It's my feeling that kids need to have this kind of focused guidance as early as eight or nine years old. Teacher friends of mine have the same observations in their classrooms when they see early signs of behavioural problems—that's when you have to nip the problem in the bud, as my grandmother used to say.

What are some signs that a kid may not be getting proper attention at home? Attention seeking in class, being hateful towards other kids, disrespecting teachers and authority, irregularly attending school, or the child's general health or appearance seems neglected, to mention a few.

I know these "symptoms" look like those of many typical, healthy youngsters, and it would probably take a massive legislative change to interfere in the home anyway, but shouldn't we be doing more to prevent kids from falling onto the wrong path? I think we should have a social support network ready for families in crisis that we as a society can use to help guide young people in the right direction. As the public continues to ignore kids who need help, the situation will become worse, and our disregard will eventually turn into a hugely expensive taxpayers' bill for keeping those neglected kids in Juvie.

I shared stories of Hank and Scott to show the importance of appropriate and balanced parenting in preparing a child for life, and to show that these kids weren't born young offenders or deserve to be 'throwaway' kids. Parents make decisions every day about their children's upbringing, and for the most part are doing a good job— after all, the vast majority of Canadian teenagers are living 'normal' lives. I think Hank and Scott's stories strongly support the idea that solid, honest, appropriate, and loving relationships provide the strongest foundation to our success as human beings by showing us what happens when familial supportive structure isn't provided.

Kyle was about thirteen or fourteen when we met after he was admitted to Juvie. He was quiet and responsive to staff during the first of his several visits to the centre. As the frequency of his admissions increased, he became familiar with being locked up and his behaviour became more obnoxious, earning him frequent time-outs. As he grew older, he told me he had fun manipulating other people—it was something he liked to do. This was rooted, as I found out later, in his childhood craving for his parents' attention, which he said for him was never enough. His father's job kept him away from home and his mother worked full-time.

His first brush with the law was the result of a typical schoolboy fight that led to vandalism on school property and damage to neighbouring homes and properties. Kyle said he became a problem child at school when he learned that "they didn't really do anything when me and my friends raised s___!" He would get the "Don't do that again" lecture and a brief suspension from school, but disciplinary action was not enough to deter him from getting into trouble. By the time he had reached Juvie, he had been living in a foster home since the age of ten or eleven.

I think that if there had been a stronger social network that could have intervened in Kyle's family life and dealt with his troublesome behaviour earlier, he may have been able to avoid the insecurity he felt and the trouble he caused in his teens.

Unfortunately we cannot press rewind and pick another path, but a comment Kyle made about his counsellors made me think. He thought that if one of them had spent some of their own time with him, he would probably have shared how he really felt about what was happening in his life. In order for him to open up, he needed someone he could trust, someone who made it seem like it was more than his or her job to be there for him. In other words, he needed someone who cared.

The damage done by unfulfilled promises, emotional neglect, lack of closeness and inconsistent parenting as described in some of these boys' stories was certainly not the whole story of their troubled lives. Some of the responsibility for their actions did lie with the boys themselves. And despite a so-called 'proper' upbringing, some kids still turned to a life of crime. I think however, that we as a society must make a concerted and ongoing commitment to intervene in family situations when necessary (no matter how young or old the child is), hold accountable both parent and child, and to assert the consequences firmly and appropriately.

As emotional creatures, people are constantly seeking an emotional balance. When kids commit severe acts of outrage and violence they are trying to ease or balance a life that is heavy with abuse or neglect or despair. I know this is an over-simplification, but as adults we can help troubled kids by giving them objective feedback with honest encouragement and attention so they can sort through their own problems. And lastly, kids want rules. Be respectful, yet firm with the rules or they won't respect you! Be fair, lead by example, encourage and compliment and most of all, listen.

I'd like to share the following letter sent to the staff at Victoria Youth Custody Centre in 1996. It was written by the grateful parents of a boy who had been in and out of our centre over a period of about two years.

September 17, 1996

To All the Staff at Victoria Youth Custody Centre,

Just a note to thank you for your care of Lou this last go around in youth custody. If my prayers get answered he will never be in custody again. Adult if he does.

We really appreciate the many things that you all did to make a difficult time easier. From the friendly hello and introducing yourself on the phone, to a quick chat when we came to visit and accommodating hours that suited our schedule. You helped so much in maintaining our family unit by keeping in touch with us through ups and downs, yours and ours. By always returning phone calls promptly, communicating your concerns and listening to ours. We felt that even though Lou and we, his family, had physical miles between us, you aided us to remain a family. It made his return home after 409 days a smoother transition.

The visiting areas being separate and semi-private with a limited number of people, is in my view a most important aspect as you can have 'real' conversations with your child. I found at Willingdon, in one large common visiting area, one is on edge and very conscious of how and what they say, even hugs are awkward. I hope if they ever build a new place they keep that visiting area like that of Victoria's.

Thank you for letting us feel as comfortable as I think one could be in a custody care situation. As 'joints' go, I'd say yours is the best run, most organized and friendliest, yet you still manage to maintain its purpose. Lou has checked out a few of them!

Thanks to the teacher who may have gotten more into the boy's head than they thought. Thanks to all for your cheerfulness and hello's. Special thanks to Glo and Gloria for their outstanding work in developing small motor skills, teaching patience, raising self-esteem and guiding some sense into his life and for taking, no, rather sharing my role as Mom. To Robb for working on the song I did for Lou. To Jim (I think they call him Jimbo) for just being him. You're a very memorable character. Does anyone ever get a straight answer from him?

Anyone I came in contact with gave me the feeling there is genuine care and concern for the kids there. I hope you will always have staff like that, and if you get one that isn't, prod them in the direction. Remember for a time in the youngsters' life, you are the bridge from a negative to a positive future. A very important role to fill, especially if they have to cross the bridge a few times. I hope Lou has finished crossing his, however if he isn't, he will be doing anymore alone.

Quick update on Lou. He has been working steady since the day after his release. Twelve-hour days, five days a week. He is learning to run an excavator in the bush. The crew stays on his case to "move with a purpose." Lou's nickname is 'Stumpy.' Anytime he can sit he finds a stump to sit on! So him, right?

It's taken quite a team to get him to adult stage. Thanks for your part, much appreciated.

Sincerely,
Lou's Parents

"This place sucks! I can't wear make-up or my own clothes or phone my boyfriend! It's the s___s!"

Those comments were from one of the seven girls involved in the Reena Virk beating and eventual death. I was supervising her and several other girls involved in the incident, along with a couple of boys not involved. We had spent the morning cleaning the building, and were sitting awaiting lunch.

The girl continued for about two or three minutes with a vehement and vulgar volley about being locked up. Suddenly, one of the boys not involved in the Virk death challenged her. Verbally, with little vulgarity and rock-solid common sense, he dumped on her with comments like: "Do you realize what you've done?", "How do you think her family feels?", "You are so self-centred, you're disgusting!", "Shut the f___ up!".

I ordered silence at this point. Just then the director, on his way to the dining room, poked his head in the door, looked around and said, "Silence is golden?" Later that day, the director asked me about the comment, and we discussed it, the timing and its effect on the kids.

The kids involved in the Reena Virk death were a difficult group to handle. Staff tried to keep them silent about the incident because it was still before the courts, and was very high profile in the community. Family visits were isolated and supervised for the most part, keeping the kids involved in the Virk case visiting alone with their families in the small visiting area in the lobby.

Kelly Ellard was a high-maintenance supervision for staff. The only boy involved, Warren Glowatski, was very quiet, very compliant with staff direction and literally faded into the background. He was also very frightened.

Suman and Manjit Virk, Reena's parents, responded positively when I asked them if they would like to express their thoughts and feelings about their experience with the youth justice system.

Here is their letter:

Critical times hard to deal with — many wonder why young children are so violent and are capable of causing great harm to others. When we do the "root cause analysis," we find that the very core of society is disintegrating fast. The "family unit" is under attack. Parents are finding it very hard to raise kids with good values. Peer pressure, commercialism and moral decadence is influencing our kids in very negative ways. Parents and adults set bad examples and are poor models for kids. Young people living under these conditions are confused and have no clear direction in life. Adolescents turn to drugs and alcohol to deal with their problems. Like-minded teens hang out aimlessly at night, vandalizing and terrorizing. Pack mentality gets them in trouble with the law. No one cares for their emotional needs and real issues. The justice system puts them through difficult steps. Some change their ways but many get desensitized and fight with the whole system. Prisons and custody and control affect them adversely. Many try to keep a tough guy image — drawing attention from other teens. Bullying brings them recognition from peers. There is lack of respect for any authority. T.V. shows belittle parents, police officers and other authority figures. These shows glamourize violence and sex. Social and justice costs are skyrocketing. Crime is a big business for the whole justice system.

Manjit and Suman Virk

2006, Victoria BC

Every visit with Warren gets better — better conversation because of both the content and the quality. Today's visit was 3 hours and 45 minutes which allowed a balanced and varied exchange in topic and in texture — more ease, more comfort with me, discussing all subjects in a more animated and personable way, as well as some actual comment about his own part in the Reena Virk tragedy.

Late spring afternoon, and I'm in conversation with Warren at Ferndale Institution near Mission in B.C.'s Fraser Valley. We've been visiting since February of this year [2004]. Warren's father was present at our visit in April. I was pleased to be included in that meeting as his father had come from San Diego, California to spend some time with his son

Paul G. strikes me as a decent man with firm opinions and an open mind. The father-son interplay was appropriate and normal and close.

Suman Virk, Reena's mother, and her husband Manjit have forgiven Warren for his part in the death of their daughter. Their reasons centred around Warren's profound effort to change his inner outlook on his life. Their comments came in a media statement following Warren's parole hearing in July of 2006, at which the Virks were present. Suman and Manjit learned that Warren had availed himself of every program available to him during the seven years of his incarceration.

Warren sat face-to-face with Reena's parents as they supported him in his request for unescorted parole into the community. Warren received seventy-two hours per month. The community learned that Warren has already been out of the institution more than 200 times in the last few years with an escort. These excursions included attendance at church, volunteer labour in parks and other local endeavours, speaking to students of criminology at various colleges, and sitting face-to-face with incarcerated young offenders.

Warren's personal efforts to change his attitudes and life outlook included participation in the creation of a video documentary called *A Healing River*. All of this and more in a sincere effort to change, to heal, to understand, to apologize and to move on in his personal life.

Support for Warren came from volunteers and professionals, personal friends and from his father. Warren's father has made a number of trips from the U.S. to be with his son. Through all of this, Warren has maintained as low a profile as is possible in this situation. He has turned down requests for interviews from Canadian and American television and Canadian radio.

"My real test will come when I'm faced with temptation somewhere in the community—and whether I can resist."

Warren's insight of himself, paraphrased here, about the positive comments on his 180° change in his personal behaviour. Realistic and grounded and acutely aware, I think Warren is a good example of what rehabilitation looks like. From *A Healing River* documentary in his own words, "get up and love someone!"

In their expressed forgiveness of Warren, the Virks have shown by example their insights into life and death and a graciousness worthy of reverence. When I approached them for this book, I was warmly received into their home, offered tea, and became much less anxious over the next hour as we conversed. Reena's younger brother and sister were playing in the other room.

Their magnamity approaches purity.

RAW VOICES V

Letter: "Lance"

Here are some sobering thoughts on the father-son relationship.
Lance wrote this letter at the age of sixteen to his father. Lance
was on remand with us at the VYCC for several months, and
had a lot of time to distill his feelings and write them down.
It's 1998.

I am writing you to let you know how angry and frustrated I
am, that you came to my court date to go against me. You
haven't been part of my life for quite a few years now, and
to be honest I do not know you very well. I have a very hard,
totally hard, time wanting anything to do with you, but on the
other hand, I have an even harder time not having anything
to do with you. You are my father and I'll never deny that, but
the way that you and mom can just vanish when things go
wrong in my life, is just not right. Man I wish I trusted you
enough to sit down with you and have a complete father-son
heart to heart talk, cause I really miss that in my life. (Not
that I ever had it before). But I know that it's something every
child needs. But the truth is I don't trust you not at all. But
I'm moving on until the day comes where you admit to all,
not just some, but all of the bulls___ you've pulled on me,
i.e. beating on me, lying, etc. You're pretty tough to beat on
a child! You can deny all this, say it's all a f___ing crock of

s_____, but I bet there's a part deep down inside you that's just rotting with guilt, but you're too proud to admit it. So next time you think, let's call me the f___-up, and preach to me and try to pull the wool over my eyes some more, don't even bother. You'll never understand me as a human being, let alone as your son, because you don't take the f___ing time! So I leave you with this: call me when you grow up. I await your phone call, but honestly I don't believe it will ever come. You've got too much to lose by admitting things about the past.

PART THREE

The Criminal
Justice System

Chapter 12   The Youth Criminal Justice Act

The original federal legislation governing youth offenders was the Juvenile Delinquents Act in effect from 1908 to 1984. The JDA provided authority for police to intervene, but left significant discretion to provinces as to setting the age of youth and disposition options. In some provinces, services to youth were a component of an overall corrections or criminal justice system (British Columbia), while in other provinces they were a component of the child welfare system (Saskatchewan).

By the 1970s, there was an evolving attitude in society that the criminal behaviour of youth was becoming more serious, with little capacity within the system to hold them accountable. There was also a concern that the child welfare system did not provide sufficient protection of the right of youth for due legal process. There was also a growing belief that there needed to be a national standard for how youth criminal behaviour was handled and on April 1, 1984, the Young Offenders Act (YOA) was legislated into law. The act standardized the definition of youth across the country as 12 to 17 years of age. It outlined the legal processes to be used, the court sanctions available, and the range of services that provinces were required to provide. It was a youth criminal justice system separate from the adult system, where the focus was on the accountability of the youth. Not only were youth considered independent of the family, the new system was separate and independent of the child welfare system. The Act also provided for federal contributions for the costs of services. However, the increase in resources through the establishment of this youth criminal justice system has not been successful in resolving the issues underlying the criminal behaviour of youth.

The Youth Criminal Justice Act replaced the Young Offenders Act as of April 1, 2003. The YCJA attempts to address some of the shortcomings of the YOA by making diversion a required service for a number of offences in order to restrict the number of youth caught up in the youth criminal justice system. It provides for some remission of custody time and transition to community resources. It provides for a more efficient transfer of youth to the adult justice system. However, it does not address the underlying issues of criminal behaviour in youth.

In the following chapters, I will share the opinions and suggestions I gathered from a wide number of professionals and caring government employees seeking to improve the level of support given to youth offenders, and the social costs of crime in the community. As a social worker friend of mine has pointed out, our society needs strong support services to assist families at risk. School-based family counselling services, readily available child and youth mental health services and enhanced child welfare services strongly linked to young offender services would help to prevent or diminish the seriousness of youth criminal behaviour. Such a shift cannot be done within only the youth criminal justice sector, but would require changes across a number of human service sectors.

RAW VOICES VI

Poem: "Doin' Time in YDC, 'Sean'"

On a lighter note, this was written by a boy who turned sixteen the day the government imposed a no-smoking ban on our centre. As a heavy smoker, Sean was really looking forward to that day in 1986!

I was standing on the corner waitin' for my man
When two dudes in blue threw me in a van
there was me and my woman sittin' on my knee
we got taken down to Vic Juvie
I'm doin' time in YDC

When I got in they strip searched me
And sent me off to closed custody
They stuck me in room number three
I gotta bang on my door just to take a pee
I'm doin' time in YDC

I wake up every morning starin' at the bricks
I can't wait till I get out so I can have my fix
I walk in the kitchen and see the cook
He always gives me a dirty look
I'm doin' time in YDC

The food here is worse than I've ever seen
I swear to God it makes your s___ turn green
Eight times a day we get a smoke
I sure wish I had a f___in' toke
I'm doin' time in YDC

They got lots of staff, they're young and old
After work they smoke Columbia Gold
I'm getting' sick and tired of hearin' keys
I gotta wash everyday unless I want scabies
I'm doin' time in YDC.

Chapter 13   The Riots and the Renos

The battering ram was about eight feet long and eight inches square. With four policemen providing the power, it was rammed against a two-inch thick door that wasn't even locked. This was riot number one for me.

It was the late seventies and I had a few years of experience in the youth justice system behind me. At the time of this riot, the centre was already in bad shape and waiting for renovations because it was an old building and we just had too many kids for the space.

The residents began the riot in the East Wing television room—a mid-sized room with concrete walls and a tile floor. There were three doors that opened into the room, including one that accessed the kitchen. I could only guess that the ringleaders of this ugly scene were the several sophisticated street teens who were tired of living in a "s____ty building" with "nothing to do!" So they 'inspired' a group of boys to barricade themselves in the television room by placing the heavy, moulded plastic couches and chairs end-to-end between the opposing doors. Because the doors were hinged to open into the room, the furniture effectively blocked entry.

At the time, this room was also the dining area, so there were circular chrome tables with more plastic chairs set around them. There was also a large bookshelf, heavy with books, and a small metal table. A sliding plywood board, locked from the kitchen side, was all that covered the pass-through from the kitchen to the television room.

Before the boys started the riot, two of us staffers were on the East Wing moving back and forth from the television room to the long hallway and the kids' rooms, attending to their needs. The centre's security policy for the East Wing was that there was only one staff member allowed in the hall at a time so the kids would never be unsupervised in the television room. But at some point the boys were able to shut us out, quickly putting the barricade in place and starting the destruction. From the other side of the door we could hear chairs smashing, tables breaking, books tearing into bits and pieces, and wooden bookshelves turning into kindling in a matter of minutes.

From the outside it sounded like a war!

As soon as the riot began, the staff called police and immediately sent the other kids to their rooms on the West Wing. All visitors were quickly ushered out of the building. We informed the director of the centre, who came in and took charge at the scene, placing an observer in the courtyard outside the television room.

Although an attempt was made to reason with the boys, it proved unsuccessful. Once the police arrived, they were in charge. For whatever reason, the kids had not blocked the pass-through door to the kitchen. The doorknob had been locked from the television room side, but was unlocked on the other side. But rather than open the door into the television room, the police and the director flattened the door with the battering ram and quickly moved in to take control of the situation.

In the aftermath of the riot, the kids involved—none of whom were injured—faced heavy consequences; the staff learned some big lessons and the government began to put new policies into place.

Of the thirteen boys involved in this fiasco, only a few remained in our centre while the others were moved to other youth custody centres in the province. The centre laid charges against some of the kids, while all who were involved faced the centre's own disciplinary action which included a 'lock down' (separation from the other kids) and having to clean up their mess. For several days the boys were busy with painting, sweeping, repairing and cleaning the destroyed television room. The kids were very quiet and respectful as they bore their punishment while the staff became much more formal in their interactions with the kids by adhering strictly to the rules, and not allowing the slightest possibility for a similar situation to happen again.

There was one other chaotic event during my career at Juvie. This one took place on the smaller West Wing, and this time there were injuries.

I heard the yelling and the banging right through the walls to where I was working on the East Wing. One of the senior staff members suddenly appeared in the television room and asked me to come with him, quickly. We ran across to the other side of the building to the West Wing that housed the girls and some of the boys.

When we got there, the staff had already locked some of the seven or eight residents in their rooms. But there were still three or four girls in the West Wing television room, and they were raising hell. Their television room was about twelve by fifteen feet, with an approximately twelve-foot sloping ceiling. One of the residents had pushed the chrome kitchen table underneath a corner shelf about five feet off the floor that usually held the television set. The television had been removed from its spot, and now a sixteen-year-old girl with long hair sat on the corner shelf, dripping with blood. From her lofty perch, she had reached the small transom window that opened to the courtyard, had broken the glass and used a shard to cut herself across the throat. Another girl was standing on the table below pleading with her distraught friend to calm down.

First the staff and I had to coax the distraught girl off the table and back to her room—which did not go smoothly. As for the girl who sat bleeding, perched over the television set, we waited for police to get her down. When the officers arrived, they asked us to get some mattresses to put on the floor below the girl in case she jumped or fell. Luckily, the police and the staff were able to talk the girl down from the shelf. She was then taken to the police station and transferred to Vancouver youth custody.

After these two major incidents, staff members attended lengthy meetings to discuss the issues arising from the incidents and how to prevent these dangerous situations from happening again. In one year, the kids had caused $200,000 worth of damage to the building! These acts of violence and destruction took an immense toll on the staff, causing more than two dozen of my co-workers to quit or leave the VYCC. For those that stayed, morale was very low, stress was rampant, and sick leave was out of control. One co-worker said to me, "As soon as I enter the building, my guts turn into a knot." Personally, I also thought of quitting.

Around this time, a boy had been digging a hole through the outside wall of his cell, keeping it hidden with a poster. He eventually escaped during a night shift. Shortly after that, all exterior walls were covered with steel plates. At one point during all this chaos, we had another kid escape from the centre. One week later, one of the staff went up to the roof to retrieve a basketball and found him—he had been camping up there in a little pup tent. When the residents found out, the staff became the laughing stock of the centre!

Apart from the structural damage to the building and escapees at this time, several residents had injured several co-workers A raging kid overturned a desk, narrowly missing a female staff member. Residents broke the arms of two more staff when they slammed their doors on them. One kid bit the thigh of a male staff member, removing some of his flesh! And, while trying to restrain another youth, a staff member slipped and had to go to the hospital to get stitches in his scalp. The stress on the staff was reaching intolerable levels, and the animosity between staff and kids was palpable.

During this time, staff met with administration to discuss the boys' riot over the poor living conditions—which was also a major complaint and concern to the staff. The building was old—built in 1963—and difficult to keep clean. The hot water heaters bolted to the walls in the kids' rooms were anchored about an inch from the wall, so over the years the residents had filled those spaces between the walls and the heaters with rotting food, filthy undergarments and other disgusting objects. The kids on the cleaning crews during day shift splashed buckets of hot water behind the heaters, both in the cells and the showers and the toilet rooms to wash the grungy refuse and smells away. Until recently the boys had pee buckets made from four-liter plastic bottles for their use overnight, but we stopped that practice after finding full pee buckets covered with green fuzz left under the beds and hidden in corners.

In our meetings with administration, we also brought up the subject of programs, and the lack thereof. The something-to-do part of living at Juvie was almost non-existent. The kids had television, one basketball hoop, string art and that was it. From time to time, some of the women on staff taught impromptu sewing and cooking classes, and male staff members supervised kids using free weights that were kept in the laundry room.

In 1979, after a considerable amount of wrangling and governmental delay, the crews came into the VYCC to begin the renovations. We had to vacate the residents from the old building so the construction guys could move in, and for about seven months we ran Juvie from an old house and Outward Bound site in Metchosin, West of Victoria. We took the kids we thought would be least likely to run away, and sent the more risky youth to Willingdon detention centre in Burnaby or placed them under house arrest with twenty-four-hour supervision.

Working at the Metchosin site was a special experience. There was one staff member for every six or seven kids and the kids received a lot of individual attention. We went on outings to a swimming pool, a beach and a speedway, we hiked in a nearby park and the kids watched a lot less television.

At Metchosin, the staff and administrative team had time to think about why the situations at VYCC were getting out of control. We discussed how staff members seemed to be all over the map in how they disciplined the troubled kids.

In the early days, some employees were good at showing the kids things to do to occupy their time—but when those staff weren't on shift, then what? There was a lack of consistency between us and our supervisors, and the kids could immediately pick up on our weaknesses. Considering the kind of attitude the kids already had in regards to the law, their natural defiance manifested daily with their "what are you gonna do about it?" kind of behaviour.

Surprisingly, while in Metchosin, the escape record was very low. And having more staff-resident activities resulted in less fighting, whining and bickering. It was also a time when staff prepared new program strategies to put in place once we moved back to the renovated building in Victoria.

However, the return to Juvie in Victoria was not all peaches and cream. One of the most basic jail fixtures are locks—locks that are strong and locks that work. When we returned to the centre, the locks had not arrived yet and the doors were also late. So when we moved back in, doors of eighteen-gauge steel were installed as a temporary measure. These doors were hollow and contained an opening for a window that was covered with stiff, wire mesh. Although the doors could close into the frame they were still easily opened because there were no locks, so on night shift when staff was down to three, we had to wedge a two-by-four across the hall against each room door. In addition, one staff member sat at the end of the hall all night to ensure security.

Once we had the new doors and new lock system in place, we could finally introduce the new programs we had been planning. Arts and crafts were back in a big way, six days a week! The kids had school five days a week and they were even asking to go! The teachers were great "kid magnets," sharing their talents and drawing these troubled and confused youngsters to their academic studies. The woodworking classes brought out special abilities in kids who didn't know they could create or build anything. These skills and personal discoveries were essential in inspiring the kids to seek post-Juvie employment. There were other benefits of having a new, upgraded centre. There were fewer conflicts among staff, residents and management and we had better morale and less stress all around.

These upgrades need to happen continually though, not just once every twenty years. Shortly after I retired from Juvie, another 'upgrade' included hiring a counsellor for the kids. I was so happy to hear that there would be a person to just listen and talk to the kids for thirty hours a week, responding to their plea, "You don't need to fix it . . . just listen to me!"

Chapter 14 Jamie's Perspective

"You're really interested in what I have to say!" said Jamie, a seventeen-year-old who experienced what life was like inside a youth custody centre in Quebec City before he got into trouble in Victoria. I interviewed Jamie at the Victoria Youth Custody Centre in 2003. Jamie was looking forward to returning to Quebec soon so he could reconnect with his mother and sister. He reminisced about the friendly, warm and outgoing people of Quebec City, likening the place to Victoria because of the cities' similarities in size, historical beauty and tourist appeal.

I met with Jamie to chat about the differences, from his point of view, between youth custody centres from one side of the country to the other. Jamie recalled that his week-long stay at the youth facility in Quebec City was for stealing chocolate bars. He estimated that the centre had 300 to 400 beds compared to the VYCC's sixty beds and he was surprised at the amount of attention the staff here in the Victoria centre gave the kids. In Quebec, he said, you got your clothing and your room and then they forgot about you. But even with that comparison, he found that the Victoria staff still didn't have much time to talk to him.

Jamie said the living conditions in the Quebec City units were rough. They had to wash up in gang showers that had curtains to separate showering, but overall there was very little privacy. Staff placed Jamie in a room with two other boys. The room contained one set of bunk beds and a single bed, typical of the rooms in the ward of about forty boys. Jamie said he definitely preferred the Victoria centre's mostly single room approach.

In Victoria, common sense guided our roommate designations. Shared rooms and bunk beds provided a good way to accommodate kids who got along and didn't cause problems for staff or other residents with excessive noise or rambunctious behaviour. And having those roommate situations encouraged the kids to talk to one another, which at times helped to relieve loneliness for a kid who could be really sinking deep into despair. I watched many friendships develop among the boys due to these roommate situations and saw that they would watch out for one another while they were socializing and in programs.

Rooming kids in Juvie is a serious matter for us to consider. Both the residents and the staff are concerned about privacy, bullying and personal hygiene. Staff and administration also had to be aware of a kid's sexual behaviour—especially if the police or courts had alerted us to problems with a particular youth—and address this issue immediately and appropriately. At the VYCC, our residency lists often carried a 'room alone' designation for a kid whose sexual behaviour or violent history required this action.

Jamie and I found that the daily routines in the Victoria and Quebec City units appeared to be pretty much the same. One of the obvious differences between these two centres was that the VYCC also housed girls, and included both male and female staff on the line. At the time when Jamie was held in the Quebec centre it was made up of male staff who watched over male residents only.

When I started at Juvie in 1976, there were men and women on staff, but female officers were only called into work when a girl was admitted. That meant if there were no female residents, female staff members would not be on shift. In the seventies, we admitted very few girls; maybe one in every six residents was female. The female residents, supervised by female officers, were segregated from the boys in a separate wing. As the years passed, more girls were admitted into custody and eventually, we were housing a greater number of kids, boys and girls. We went from considering eight or ten kids as a high residency count to getting used to twenty being the average.

There was also another change that was gradually appearing behind our doors. In the early years of my work at the VYCC, the minority racial group, which was about one in five kids, was First Nations. As the Canadian population changed, Juvie began to reflect the communities outside its walls. So along with Caucasian and First Nations kids, we were also admitting kids of Vietnamese, Chinese, Japanese, Filipino and East Indian backgrounds, along with a few kids whose roots were from Jamaica, Africa and the Middle East.

One thing I noticed was that although the ethnic makeup of the kids became more diverse over the years, the ethnic composition of the staff did not change as swiftly. Having a racially diverse staff would be an ideal arrangement in youth custody centres. Just like placing a female officer with a female inmate, kids identify with staff members who share some commonality with them. This makes the residents more comfortable and open to communicate, which is good for keeping the peace.

Having staff composed of both men and women offered additional benefits. We found that it was helpful to show the residents that men and women were able to communicate and work well together. Besides, I had lots of fun working with most of my female colleagues. I always looked forward to being on the same shift with them as they brought a refreshing attitude to that high-testosterone place. Many of the kids we worked with came from dysfunctional families where the mom or the dad was seen as the 'enemy.' Having both male and female staff members ensured that if a boy had issues with men, there would be a woman available to talk with him and vice-versa. In addition, boys were more likely to challenge a man physically in order to save face in front of their peers, but did not feel threatened or embarrassed when a female officer talked them out of a fight. But when some of the residents' arguments came down to fisticuffs, female staff members would jump in to break it up just as often as their male colleagues.

On a more serious note, the administration also encouraged the composition of mixed gender staff in order to keep a close watch on any suspicious romantic or sexual interactions between male residents and female staff, or between female residents and male staff. Having both women and men on watch helped prevent the possibility of an inappropriate situation developing between the kids and their adult supervisors.

In addition to the correctional institutions' debates over same- or mixed-gender facilities, administration and staff were also very interested in segregating units for those residents on remand (waiting in custody to appear in court) and for those in sentence housing (serving their court-imposed incarceration).

In 2003, I visited an institution in Western Australia that separately houses young offenders who are on remand and those who were serving their sentence. My four-hour visit to the Rangeview Remand centre, a seventy-two bed centre just outside of Perth, gave me a new perspective on the VYCC, and I learned that we share many of the same problems such as male/female issues, housing within the centre, how to mete out discipline, funding, and the day-to-day issues with the kids themselves.

During our interview, Jamie continued to compare Victoria and Quebec City's programs. Both centres offered outdoor and indoor basketball and, of course, school, woodworking, and arts and crafts activities. He thought the kids should have more choices about how they spent their time in custody. For example, he believed residents should be allowed to go outside more, to see "lots of trees and birds in the outdoors." That's very true, I agreed, remembering how the kids' attitudes had changed for the better when the VYCC was temporarily located in Metchosin.

Chapter 15   Jean, Veteran Caregiver

"I am their caregiver, not their parent. They have their own parents!" said Jean, who has given over twenty-five years of love and discipline to some of the most violent and disturbed teenagers in British Columbia.

When signing government forms, Jean crosses out 'Foster Parent' and writes 'Caregiver' next to her name because she wants to make it clear that the troubled kids that she looks after have their own parents—even though some of those did not deserve to be parents. Jean houses and supervises boys from age twelve to seventeen years when it is not safe for them to live in their own homes.

Over the past twenty-five years, our paths have crossed a number of times as many of the same boys who lived with her also did some time in the Victoria Youth Custody Centre. I have visited her home and met her family, and have always been impressed by her sense of integrity and support. Jean is a goldmine. Social workers view her as a no-nonsense, firm, fair, nurturing and highly respected caregiver who is a credit to her community.

At a table in a quiet corner of a restaurant, Jean and I met to talk about youth in conflict from her point of view.

Compared to the teenagers under her care twenty years ago, Jean said the kids today have to want help to get any help. They get so caught up in saying "What's the use?" that they stay in a rut, always going back to the streets, always going back to crime. But to find a better life, Jean believes the kids have to avoid the street life, stay away from what they thought was normal, and just try something different, either through living in a good foster home or participating in a good alternative program like Outward Bound. Jean noted that teenagers today often need to have to make those decisions on their own because the government has drastically cut the resources for kids in conflict with the law.

Since the eighties, the system has focused on better health and education for troubled kids. As Jean points out, the kids out there are more sophisticated in their approach to things. They're street-savvy. They have gangs. They are more materialistic, asserting their independence with their clothes—like shiny tracksuits and flashy jewelry. They don't see how the system can help them.

"They're exactly who they say they are," said Jean. "They're difficult kids. They are not trustworthy. They resist anything they think you're imposing on them. I have a boy right now who says he's not going to quit smoking. He is thirteen years old and he says, 'I smoke a pack a day, I have always smoked a pack a day since I was a nine,' period. He doesn't care if he has asthma, as long as he has his independence."

But as a caregiver, Jean believes it's her job to look below the surface of a kid's seemingly troubled, unhealthy and uncaring attitude to find the "real beautiful person" beneath the tough exterior. She compares this philosophy to a boy whose teeth need fixing—with braces and time he will have a new smile and even a new attitude. As an example, Jean noticed that one of her boys had a talent for running so she made sure to encourage him, telling him he was a good athlete. This support certainly went the extra mile because not only did he start to respect his gift as a runner, his school grades also moved up two levels! "That kid's walking tall now," Jean recalled. "He's got a girlfriend and he's just being a normal kid."

We didn't talk for very long about the problems in British Columbia's foster care system, but we did discuss the ramifications of overburdened social workers passing along their cases to other colleagues.

Social workers do not receive a lot of extra help in the form of an assistant or supervisor. When social workers' caseloads become too much for them to handle, they are expected to find someone else to take the overflow. Sometimes youth files are passed along from one social worker to another, many times over. This creates a disruptive pattern of strangers entering a family's life who are not familiar with the history and specific needs of the child. This is frustrating for both the child and the caregiver, and makes change and support a slow and confusing process.

Jean spoke about an alternative and controversial approach to reducing the risk of kids becoming young offenders. She suggested that youth workers should be in the homes working directly with the parents. However, it's unlikely that most parents of troubled kids would say they want youth workers in their homes because as far as they're concerned, their child is fine. Some parents don't see any problems in their home even though their daughter may have been arrested four or five times for drugs or violence.

"And you're telling me there's nothing wrong there?" Jean asked. "That's crazy."

"Do you mean a professional should go into those homes and intervene when domestic problems appear?" I asked.

"Yeah, but can you imagine what kind of opposition there would be to that?" Jean snickered. "Parents would complain that the government would be infringing on their rights to raise their child, and so on."

But what can you do when a child is growing up in an unstable home? The social workers' hands are tied until something serious happens. They've got to follow protocol, and they just can't step in as quickly as they would like to. Just as a new system is put into place, and the youth workers adjust to new laws and policies, a new government is elected and policies change again. However, Jean is honest about the effects of the system's constantly changing rules and standards: "We have to adjust, and sometimes we go backwards and sometimes we go forwards."

I broached a different topic that I had been curious about and asked Jean what her biggest concern was in regards to the government's attitude or treatment of foster parents. Jean said she has never been treated disrespectfully. Only once has she been involved in a tense situation with a social worker who had demanded that Jean accept a very troubled kid who was likely to disobey her house rules. Jean said no to the social worker's request and refused to accept the boy into her home.

Jean is tough. She does not allow the kids under her care to bring drugs or alcohol into the house, and bans both smoking and cigarette possession on the premises. She said she has to draw a clear line with her house rules otherwise the kids—and the social workers—won't respect her or the values she is trying to teach them.

"Why should kids have values?" I asked.

"Why do we have a heart? It keeps us living. Without values we're nothing; if you have no values you have no self-esteem."

Jean agrees that some troubled kids have warped values, but with time and support they can learn that those values aren't helpful and will take steps to change them. "Kids learn what it takes to feel genuinely good about themselves, and if their values make them or others feel crappy, then eventually those values have to change if they want to change."

"What would you do to change things to make your job better?" I asked.

"Money is an issue, but the more money you have, the more

you spend," Jean said thoughtfully. "The thing is, if I could have two of me I could cover all my bases perfectly."

However, unless she feels like she's putting in 150 percent effort, she worries that the government will get someone else to look after her foster kids—and she doesn't want 'new people' looking after her kids.

"I'm really fanatical that way," she said. "Some of these kids are so delicate . . . "

Jean recognizes that she does need to know when to ask for help, and often that help is calling on the ministry for assistance.

I asked her what it took to be a good foster parent.

"You've got to really, really like it—no matter what they do to you." Jean said. "You've got to really care about them or you just don't make it and they don't make it—you have to go that last mile for them."

Jean was raised in northern Alberta, where her father sexually and physically abused her. After her parents divorced, Jean lived with her grandmother, who taught her how to heal from years of abuse.

"How did you heal?" I asked.

"You forgive them," she replied immediately. She said she had learned how to appreciate life, no matter how bad, the situation.

Jean has a family of her own and I asked her what effect having foster kids in her house had on her husband and children. She said her husband was very supportive, and didn't take what the kids did personally. Her son and daughter, now in their thirties, had learned the truth about what life can be like for some kids "and the reality out there." Jean also spoke of the mutual respect she shares with her family, saying that family members are allowed the freedom to become involved in their own interests, separate from shared activities with the foster kids. She said that the support and love of her family is what recharges her emotional batteries, allowing her to be there for the emotional needs of her foster kids.

Without a doubt, Jean said, everything she experienced as an abused child provided her with the knowledge and wisdom to deal with her foster kids. Sometimes, experiencing horrible situations can teach a person what not to do in life. That was how Jean approached parenthood.

"Because I was abused, I knew there was no way I was going to bring abuse to my children."

Jean said that the high point of her career is "getting these kids in touch with themselves—that's a reward worth more than money."

I asked if she was in touch on a regular basis with other caregivers. She replied bluntly that she used to go to the coffee parties and listen to the constant complaints of her colleagues, but then stopped going.

"Foster parents have got to get off their ass and do something for themselves, and that's the bottom line. You cannot be sitting there collecting your cheque and expecting somebody to lay out the whole program for you. When kids come in, get to know them on a personal level. The first day a kid enters my place, we go out and buy brand new sheets, a brand new mattress, a brand new quilt and a brand new pillow in the colour they want, and for once in their life they have something that belongs to them. It's personal. Then when they leave they can take their bedding and pillow. I do it for my own biological kids, so why wouldn't I do it for my foster kids?"

"What do the kids call you?"

"Bitch!" Jean chuckled. "Sometimes 'Mom' but that sort of slides off the cuff. They usually just call me Jean."

I asked Jean what her feeling was about being included in this book.

"It scares the s___ outta me!" she replied instantly, and then she elaborated. "You know Gord, we're talking about so many of the more important things in life than the experiences I've had. Sometimes I think what the hell am I doing? I don't think a lot of people like me, that's why I don't have a whole lot of acquaintances. I almost feel like I'm on the outside of the circle with adults, but with kids I'm right in there. I feel really comfortable inside that circle." She added that it was tough to sit with me and talk about the truth of her job.

"But you do it all day with the kids," I said.

"But not with 'adults'," Jean responded. "I just relate better to children."

She added, "I get frustrated when I look at dysfunctional parents and I think, oh my God, where were your mom and dad? I become very protective of the kids and their emotions. I could not go into corrections and do your job, Gord. I have to be there to walk the kids through their emotions. 'Did you feel bad when your dog died, or when your mom put you down? Don't worry, it'll come to pass. Seize the moment.' At five-minutes-to-one that kid can be so bad, and at three-minutes-past-one they think you're the most wonderful person in the world. Those minutes between are so delicate to them."

To be a caregiver, Jean believes you have to be prepared to go on an incredible life journey, but it's a journey that not many people want to take. "Sometimes I don't know how I put up with all this," she said, but agreed it was a privilege to share her life with these troubled kids. Jean confided that there have been times when she hasn't always felt their pain, and she hasn't always had sympathy for where they were coming from, but she always goes to bat for them because they all have a place in her heart.

"Any regrets?"

"None."

RAW VOICES VII

Letter: "Brett"

"Inmate writing paper" titles this page. It's another ex-resident contemplating life in the late '70s.

I was very happy to receive your letter. You expressed something a lot of people never have and that is about not having a father. You are right as I did miss my dad. I try to follow in my oldest brother's footsteps but then I just try and play a role... I never felt anything about the people I hurt. I received six months and two year's probation plus a thousand dollar fine...

I thank you for your letter it did a lot for me, brought up a lot of things I held back. Thank you.

From Wilkinson Road Provincial Jail on Vancouver Island.

Chapter 16   Stan Hyatt, Director

The youth custody centre in Prince George, British Columbia, is almost 800 kilometres north of Vancouver. In this city of over 77,000 people, nestled in a valley where the Fraser and Nechako Rivers join in their run to the Pacific Ocean, I spoke with Stan Hyatt more than a decade into his reign as the Director of the Prince George Youth Custody Centre (PGYCC).

Stan teased me about driving in the middle of winter, through wind and snow, to interview him for the book. The PGYCC is a thirty-six-bed facility that includes secure custody on the main campus and open custody units at its nearby Bowron House. Bowron is a halfway house of handpicked residents who are able to function appropriately and consistently in the community while serving the conditions of their sentences. I thought having a halfway house on the property was a great way to offer alternative rehabilitation to kids.

"You may think I'm innovative, but some of the stuff we do here, you can't do in an urban centre," said Stan.

He cautioned me the results could be different in places like Vancouver or Burnaby because the types of kids living in the big city are different from those living elsewhere in the province. In Prince George, there are more aboriginal kids, more rural communities and more naïve young people who just don't have the street smarts of city kids.

He elaborated, "In the big cities, you have the gang kids. When we get them up here [in the detention centre] some of the stuff we try with them doesn't work." He said the centre needs to have those hard-edged city kids for a long period of time before the staff and its programs can break down the kids' tough barriers.

Stan said 90 percent of the kids who come to the centre have had no family support so it's the staff's job to provide that while the kids are residents. He believes there are many custody centres doing a good job providing the same support, but he acknowledges that it is important that there be a safety net for the kids once they get out.

"Unless we link them with good people, agencies and volunteers it's not going to work, no matter where they come from."

Who do you connect them with? I asked.

Stan said they try for any volunteer program in Prince George, from Meals on Wheels to seniors' centres. The PGYCC has a family membership at the local YMCA so the residents can meet different people and learn what it's like to be healthy and fit and how to incorporate that into their lifestyle. These community programs work and Stan has seen these kids going to the YMCA or the library long after they've been released from custody.

"What is the minimum time a kid should be in the centre for its programs to have an effect on the kids?"

"Six to nine months," was Stan's reply. Unfortunately, the new Youth Criminal Justice Act of 2003 discourages keeping kids that long. "So the worst thing, and you'll hear this from a lot of other directors," said Stan, "is they're coming back because they were here for a very short period of time and we didn't get a chance to work with them."

Because of these time limits, the centre's rehabilitation program does not have the chance to work with the more serious youth offenders in encouraging them to change their ways. "So a lot of those kids do very little while they're here," said Stan. "Then they go right back to their old ways when they get out. We've had more success with the longer-term kids." He was referring to the kids who had served sentences of two to three years under the earlier Young Offenders Act (1984–2003).

Stan has noticed that the YCJA deters judges from sending 'soft criminals' to PGYCC because it is seen as a secure custody centre. Unlike jail, however, his centre does not enforce a punitive attitude.

"It's a good chance for kids to turn their lives around and I don't think that's a general perception nationally. I think politicians are trying to keep kids out of jail, which I think is good, but in other ways a place like this is good. [The PGYCC] helps the kids but we don't have them long enough. The kid with the longest sentence we've had is for eight months' jail, the average sentences are around thirty to sixty days."

Under the YCJA, the sentencing of youth offenders incorporates conditional releases. Stan noted that most of these kids are released after serving two-thirds of their sentence inside a detention centre, but then about 75 percent of released kids return to the centre for the rest of their sentence as a result of not meeting the conditions imposed while they were out. The new Act was set up to provide a nice transition to the community during the last third of their sentence, but the kids aren't buying into it.

"If the kids are in for only a short stay—twenty days—they are not interested in programs," said Stan. "[The kids will say,] 'Let me do my twenty days and I'm out.' Unless we get the kids for a long period of time, we don't have much success."

The Youth Criminal Justice Act (April 2003) emphasizes diversion before detention. It offers police more discretion to divert an offending youth to a community-based program.

These programs would include community hours in volunteer organizations, restorative justice and counselling programs. Police have always had the ability to divert, but incarceration occurs for more serious indictable offences such as violence against a person, assault and of course, manslaughter and murder charges.

I asked Stan what his greatest concern was concerning youth justice. He replied that he finds the current laws which encourage letting kids out of their incarceration two-thirds of the way through their sentence stop them from getting proper help. For example, if a girl is referred to a detox program but, because of the law, is let out for release in the last third of her sentence it is unlikely that she will make it through the program. However, in order to increase certain sentences up to two to three years, there is a huge amount of paperwork required that is tied up in the legal world.

Stan was frustrated that over the years many excellent programs within the community had been set up, and yet the centre did not have the kids in custody long enough to use the programs. He said that jails are now strictly punitive with little opportunity to rehabilitate. He added that because police are not charging young offenders the way they used to, youth crime statistics have dropped and this can mislead the courts in their sentencing.

"When directors get together, what's on the agenda?" I asked.

"More than ever, we're all on the same page now because we only have three centres [that are secure custody in BC] and we're all trying to make sure we provide a pretty good array of programs. We have three or four basic areas that we're looking at: open custody—trying to make sure we're as open as possible with the kids we've got and we're looking at transitional programs; we're also focusing on aboriginal issues—how we can try and prevent the over-representation of aboriginals in our centres; and we also talk about staff training—we want to make sure we deliver this quality product as best we can."

Stan said they were also getting involved with a new provincial implementation of international standards and accreditation. At the time of our meeting, British Columbia was the only province participating in this initiative. A council on accreditation based in New York City had initiated this project to enable the administration of youth custody centres, once they have been accredited, to justify their behaviours and their procedures to anyone who may wish to criticize. This would replace the old methods of inspections and standards, when government officials would come into the centres and tell them to improve mundane things like changing light bulbs.

According to Stan, "[the inspection officials] never talked to the kids or the staff about a program, so no one measured what we did."

The new council will change that. He outlined how each centre would have a quality improvement team made up of line staff. Instead of having outsiders come in to recommend changes, this new group would submit reports to management that would suggest improvements to the supervision and handling of the residents. The residents would also have input on an ongoing basis.

Stan Hyatt is obviously a man suited for his job and enjoys the work he has chosen. He has a reputation for encouraging and supporting the men and women he supervises, and his innovative approach to directing youth centres has raised and maintained the morale in the centre, exemplifying an admirable leadership style.

"We're responsible for protecting the community, plus we're responsible for rehabilitating the kids that come here, that's the director's job, and we have to balance both of these things," said Stan. "So we have to find the lines where we're not jeopardizing the community and we're rehabilitating those kids, and in a rural setting, we have a terrific opportunity to get those kids back in a community and that's what we try and do here."

Chapter 17   Chuck Cadman, Member of Parliament

"Was I angry? Goddamned right I was angry!" said the silver-haired Chuck Cadman, former Member of Parliament (from 1997-2005) for Surrey North.

In 1992, a group of teenagers had randomly attacked Chuck's sixteen-year-old son Jesse, stabbing him to death—but only one boy out of the six who attacked him was charged with murder. Now, as we sat together in his constituency office one spring afternoon in 2003, Chuck talked to me about how his anger and grief over Jesse's death had changed his life. He had felt compelled to steer his life path into politics to push for changes in the youth justice system. "To me, it made a hell of a lot more sense to take that energy of what I was feeling, all that anger, and put it in some direction that was going to at least help me, you know, because you have to help yourself in dealing with the consequences so other parents shouldn't have to bury their child, especially when their death is caused intentionally by somebody else."

Behind the scenes on Parliament Hill in Ottawa, Cadman was a strong advocate of diversion programs—community work that young offenders completed as part of their sentence outside of jail. In his riding back on the West Coast, he also spoke to school groups about youth and crime, holding assemblies of ten- to eighteen-year-olds spellbound as he shared his family's devastating story of Jesse's murder. His natural, down-to-earth attitude made the people of his Surrey North riding, as well as officials in the Canadian youth justice system, trust his leadership and plans for change. At the time we met for our interviews, he exuded a sense of both strength and vulnerability as he was undergoing cancer treatment while serving as an MP, husband and father to his daughter.

I asked Chuck what he considered to be the worst thing about the current juvenile system and he said that there was a complete lack of consequences for kids when they first break the law. "They should have to deal immediately with a judge's swift punishment for their crimes."

I had heard this opinion before. Back in the late seventies, I had spoken to a judge who had told me, "Three weeks should be the maximum amount of time from when they commit the crime to when they stand before me in court; but I've had juveniles before me in court six months after their crime who couldn't remember what they were being punished for!"

Cadman shared the concerns with the youth corrections system. "Now nothing happens if there's an FTA (failure to appear in court)—the judge just responds to that by saying to the kid, 'Just make sure you're here next week.' What the hell is that?" Chuck asked, spitting out the words in frustration. "What message is that, when a judge just told the boy that he can do an FTA without any consequence? To be a kid, to be a teenager, is all about learning the consequences for going past your limits!"

"Getting away with something like an FTA just makes it look okay when it's not," I agreed.

"Yeah."

The thing that got Chuck's attention after Jesse was murdered was the courts' failure in getting parents to comply with Section 7.1 of the Young Offenders Act known as "Placement of young person in care of responsible person." This section required parents or guardians of young offenders to assume responsibility for making sure their kids don't break the rules of their probation. Chuck knew the weakness of Section 7.1 all too well because the boy convicted for Jesse's murder was a young offender on probation who wasn't even supposed to leave his home, and if he did leave, it was only with his father's supervision.

Cadman asked me the same question his family and friends have been asking since Jesse's death, "So where the hell was the boy's father the night his kid murdered Jesse?"

For three months after the boy had been released from Juvie into his father's custody the youth was busting curfew every night. "Where the hell was the father?" Cadman asked. "Something should have happened to his father."

In an attempt to find the answers to these upsetting questions, Chuck went into politics to change that one section of the Young Offenders Act (YOA) that had failed to protect his son's life. Before the YCJA came into effect in 2003, Chuck had to do some head-butting in Parliament to push for this change. According to Cadman, Anne McLellan, the Minister of Justice and Attorney General of Canada, had agreed to his proposed changes to Section 7.1, thus making supervising adults more accountable for youths' behaviour.

The opposition argued that Cadman was trying to make the parent accountable for the crimes of the child. But Chuck countered their debate by saying the supervising parents or guardians should be held accountable if they failed to comply with their legal duty to supervise their children. The young offender who killed Jesse Cadman should have been under his father's supervision at the time the killing occurred. Under the old YOA legislation, there was no consequence for the father's lack of supervision. As a result of Chuck Cadman's initiative, there are now consequences for the non-compliant parent under the Youth Criminal Justice Act.

Even before Jesse's death, Chuck knew that there were problems in the juvenile justice system. The parliamentarian remembered hearing about a killing in Surrey three months before his son had died. He recalled, "I started getting stirred mostly about the murderer's sentence. I was asking myself, "What is this? The kid goes out and murders and only gets three years? What kind of consequence is that?"

His son's murderer was three weeks away from turning seventeen when he killed Jesse, so the court convicted him as an adult and the judge gave the teen a life sentence which meant at least five to ten years behind bars before eligibility to apply for parole.

To help deal with his anger and grief, Chuck began speaking to school groups about his family's experience the first few years following Jesse's killing. His presentations brought teachers, parents and kids to tears. He'd go to school after school, showing them a video his family made about their deeply painful grief still present three years after his son's death. The students watched his wife talk about the empty feeling she felt every single night when she went to bed. His daughter recalled the first night of her brother's death, when she felt that her house wasn't her home anymore.

It was from here, making a difference at the community level that led Chuck to take his impassioned voice to audiences on the federal level. He advocated that early intervention in troubled kids' lives was the key. Kids don't suddenly become killers at the age of thirteen. Often, an abusive family life is responsible for hardening children's emotions, making them desperate to hurt others as a way to relieve their own pain.

Chuck couldn't begin the process of grieving for a long time because he became so overwhelmed with the justice system.

"With all the s___ of the 'cops 'n' courts' scene, of hearing this then that, I wasn't finding the time to deal with the eternal, to deal with the grief."

But Chuck wasn't looking for pity. He wanted understanding—from his young school audiences, his colleagues on Parliament Hill and from the courts. He wanted everyone to understand that the ramifications of violence go on and on and on for victims and their families long after news of the crime disappears from the front pages of the newspapers. Cadman wanted people to know about the "walking wounded out there" and how some never recover from the grief. The frustration with a legal system incapable of handing out sufficient punishment or offering long-term rehabilitation for its young criminals can also debilitate a person's well being, often preventing closure to a horrendous ordeal.

At the time as I was first meeting with Chuck, the young man who took Jesse's life one October night eleven years before was now sitting across the country in solitary confinement. After his conviction he was sent to the Kent maximum-security penitentiary in the upper Fraser Valley of British Columbia, where he tried to kill himself. He was then shipped out to the Donnacona maximum security institution outside of Quebec City, where he caused a lockdown and got into trouble with other inmates and the staff. This resulted in his being sent to a prison where he is held in segregation, and allowed out of his cell for only one hour a day.

At his school presentations, Chuck shared details of the young man's life in prison and would warn the kids of the gradual effects of bullying and youth violence. According to Chuck, the 'bottom line' was to get kids to understand that a youth's criminal actions doesn't just affect the life of his victim, but that the offender's life too is also destroyed in the process.

"Jesse's murderer's life is now completely shot," Cadman said, "because he hasn't shown any attempt to deal with his issues while he's been in prison."

The public's frustration with the youth justice system comes from watching the news and hearing about how some kid had done something completely over the top and then basically gotten away with the crime. But as far as Cadman was concerned, there was room in the system for better rehabilitation.

Chuck explained that the new Youth Criminal Justice Act deals more with 'extrajudicial' (outside of the court) issues like diversion programs. These programs enable young offenders to do their time in the community working in logging camps or on fishing boats or participating in wilderness survival programs. If offenders become productive members of society, then that is perhaps all that we can hope for, but Cadman also believed that there should be serious consequences for young offenders who kill.

Chuck acknowledged that the Youth Criminal Justice Act wasn't perfect because it doesn't address the issue of juveniles who commit murder being automatically transferred to adult court. The new YCJA states that all trials will now be in youth court first, without the former initial hearing to decide if the trial should go to adult court (as was practiced under the old Young Offenders Act).

At the present time, it is only when the trial is over that the court decides whether the youth will be sentenced as an adult or as a juvenile. Cadman said many people in the country want to see young murderers treated as adult criminals with judges hammering down hefty life sentences instead of a "feathery" six-year sentence for second-degree murder or a ten-year sentence for first-degree murder.

Chuck said that in his opinion—an opinion shared by the justice committee who recommended changes to the new Youth Criminal Justice Act—he would have also liked to see the minimum age of kids convicted under the YCJA lowered to ten and the upper age limit be lowered to sixteen. But the biggest problem Chuck had with the new Act was that it was three times longer and about ten times more complicated than the old Act. "It's filled with all kinds of shoulds and mays and not enough shalls and wills. And that tells me there's going to be lots of work for lawyers!"

With these complexities in the new YCJA, Chuck predicted that now the time from when a youth is caught for a crime to when he stands before the judge for sentencing will be more like six months to a year.

When talking to adult audiences, Chuck asks parents to think about their responsibilities. It's up to them to teach their children respect and the value of authority. Parents can't afford to be negligent or allow their kids to get out of control. Chuck and I both agreed that even so much as a furrowed brow and a scowl from our fathers was all that most times seemed to be necessary to keep us on the straight and narrow.

"We were all sixteen once, and part of growing up is getting into s___, pushing the limits," Cadman said. "But what a society has to do is set the limits and make sure they're respected so that when kids do wander outside of them, something happens to bring them back in for good."

At the end of our last meeting, we shook hands. We had developed a friendship based on our common views and our concerns with the youth justice system. I asked him how his cancer treatment was going and he said, "It seems to be doing well and I will be heading back to Ottawa soon."

Chuck Cadman passed away a few months later in July of 2005 from a two-year fight with cancer, leaving Canadians with an indelible memory of a good and decent man who transformed his grief into a quest for youth justice for all victims.

Chapter 18   Rick Schwartz, Lawyer

Rick Schwartz, former chair of the Youth Justice section of the Canadian Bar Association and a lawyer who has worked in the youth criminal courts of Victoria since the early eighties, invited me to his office to have a discussion during his lunch break.

Schwartz is friendly and very approachable and I was impressed that he adjusted his schedule in order to speak to me about his experiences. I thought he looked very 'lawyerish' with his suit, spectacles and enviable head of dark hair. At the time we met, the federal government had recently replaced the Young Offenders Act with the new Youth Criminal Justice Act and so our discussion opened up with some shop talk.

Rick, being the lawyer he is, had a few astute and critical words about the YCJA. "It's incredibly complex. It's a badly drafted act but eventually everyone in the system will get used to it, and not remember its complexity was ever a problem."

But, I asked, does it answer the questions about what to do with kids in trouble? From Rick's point of view, the YCJA provides more guidance than the previous act about how to deal with the less serious offenders, and about the need to have alternative programs to keep kids out of custody who don't need to be there.

I agreed with Rick's support for more laws for alternative sentencing like diversion programs. This type of sentencing seems to be a more economical and beneficial way to keep kids, especially new offenders, away from the 'school of crime' custody centres and little rehabilitation, followed by yet more crime. Diversion programs have taught kids to be more responsible for their actions by putting them in real-life scenarios. Youth learn quickly that they are accountable for their troublemaking, and when they break the rules, they will be punished.

Rick suggested another way that a youth offender could serve his or her time. "There's another interesting option—the ISSP (Intensive Support and Supervision Program) provides courts with one further route to try and avoid jail for a serious offender." Under the ISSP, a correctional officer would be able to check up on residents who are on probation. However, as Rick pointed out, the scare tactic of surprise checkups probably wouldn't help convince young offenders that a life of crime was not a worthy route to follow.

Rick and I also got onto the testy subject of adult court for young offenders, a subject which Chuck Cadman and I had discussed earlier. Schwartz said the new YCJA has changed the procedures of raising a youth to adult court in a very positive way. He saw the controversial amendment in the new act from a lawyer's perspective.

Under the old Young Offenders Act, in order to raise a kid to adult court, lawyers would have to add a hearing before any trial or disposition of charges that would decide whether or not that case should go to adult court. Rick explained that under the YOA, judges and lawyers were in unenviable positions because at these hearings, they would have to try to make predictions about the most suitable consequences for kids before they would go on trial, before knowing the full extent of the crimes. Plus, he said, sentencing a sixteen- or seventeen-year-old to adult prison, among hardened, jaded, remorseless and hardcore criminals who abusively haze new inmates, is a scary prospect for any judge or lawyer to consider. Under the new Youth Criminal Justice Act, the courts can deal with what the kid did, at the trial, without having to hold the hearing before the trial to argue whether or not he or she should be sentenced as an adult or a youth

As Rick finished his lunch, we progressed into the subject of his day-to-day frustrations in dealing with teens and the law. He said the most frustrating thing about his work was that he deals with kids who so often come from screwed-up circumstances like family abuse or neglect.

"They have no chance," he said. "And then judges, lawyers and social workers have to deal with these kids in a way that requires them to overcome their upbringing in a very short period of time, or else they get more and more punishment. So it's frustrating to deal with kids who are so deprived, and have so few assets to try to help them stay out of court and out of trouble—whether it be emotional, family or financial trouble."

Rick suggested that now the main work of the court beyond dealing with the offence charges is "getting the kid dealt with in a way which is hopefully fair, respectful of their legal rights, but also in a way which hopefully does something toward reducing the likelihood that they are going to come back to court."

He said that you have got to provide support for kids from an early age to make sure they don't grow up to be criminals. Many of the serious repeat offenders can probably be identified from their behaviour from when they were in kindergarten.

"You can see which children are able to sit still, are able to concentrate, are able to try to learn to read, and are able to relate well with their peers," he said. "It is children who are not able to show these kinds of normal behaviours that need more support from the government to ensure that they get the proper mental, emotional, and social support they may be missing at home."

Rick finds it frustrating to watch governments cut back on providing social services to families and schools that need more support at home and in the classrooms. These early years of support and professional counselling are important for children and families in need. Kids in trouble also need to have 'pro-social' (or mentoring) contact with youth care workers and other adults.

"If you don't provide those opportunities for kids," he said, "the less likely you're going to be able to divert abnormal behaviours."

I asked Rick if he thought whether we had progressed in a positive way with youth and the law since the days of the Juvenile Delinquents Act, which was written in 1908 and replaced in 1984 with the Young Offenders Act, and then again with the Youth Criminal Justice Act in 2003.

Schwartz pondered the question before replying. "Society is far more rights-oriented and procedurally-oriented for all good reasons; far more now than in the 1920s. The Juvenile Delinquents Act certainly needed updating in relation to equality rights, procedural rights, and rights to counsel formal protections of the law. The YOA addressed that in a sufficient manner, so we've progressed in a formal procedural way, and that's a positive thing."

He said that an interesting thing about the new YCJA is that it permits redirection of 'discretion' back out into the community — meaning that municipalities, towns, villages, and neighbourhood police can deal more directly with those early offenders. And that's a positive move, he said, because many of the kids just need to be brought home in a police car for them to get the message, and for their families to get the message.

"I remember being brought home by a police car," Rick

recalled. "I got caught doing the kind of stuff that everybody did. Sometimes it [bad behaviour] is just bad luck. I don't think I needed the full force of the youth criminal justice system applied to me—all I needed was a bit of a wake-up call, and that's what the YCJA Act stresses is appropriate in many cases, so that's a good move."

I asked Rick what he thought about the viewpoint of "lock 'em up and throw away the key."

"Wait 'til it's their own kid!" was Rick's immediate response. "That's a view that I find doesn't withstand any amount of education or experience."

In his experience, the only people supporting that viewpoint were those who had been a direct victim of a young offender. Their hunger for revenge can override compassion or sympathy. Sometimes learning about a young offender's violent childhood alters the victim's perspective.

Officials and the government are always in debate over how many kids should be held in the youth custody centres. There are certainly arguments to be presented for both larger and smaller institutions. From my own experience, I think that thirty to forty resident beds is the best number for the economics of the corrections system, for running rehabilitation programs that work and to maintain healthy staff morale so they can provide those 'pro-social' interactions with the kids.

At the time of our meeting, Rick went on to say that he was impressed with the new Victoria Youth Custody Centre, which was now a forty-eight bed facility. He found its open wing concept with the cells facing into the common area (so kids weren't directly across the hall from each other) offered more privacy to the residents and created a homey feel. He also agreed with the concept of having separate buildings for school, program areas and administration offices, along with a private building for kids dealing with psychiatric and psychological problems. These were good solutions for "making a big institution feel small."

I remembered when staff and kids would organize mock court sessions. We re-created each 'court' with lawyers, bailiffs, witnesses and judges who handed down consequences onto the young defendants. While watching the kids act out their impression of court justice, I would notice how the mock judges' sentencing was usually fair—but tougher than those handed out by the real judges. Prompted by this memory, I flipped the other side of the sentencing coin and asked Schwartz, "Are judges using the full extent of the laws they have available to them, or are they too lenient?"

Rick was eager to address this notion of judges being too lenient. "To an uninformed observer they may appear too lenient, or to an uninformed observer they may appear too harsh, so it's really important that critics be informed about what they're talking about." He added that everyone has a right to an opinion but said, "I think some people don't deserve to have an opinion, because they don't have any experience to base it on."

Rick also commented on the courts' present-day flexibility in sentencing. "For example, a youth can get an adult court life sentence but with a shorter minimum period of jail time before he or she becomes eligible for parole. So in my view, the courts have plenty of power, plenty of options."

Rick has not had to appeal many sentences. He agrees that most of the judges' decisions are well within the range of what's acceptable, although he was often frustrated when different judges sentenced similar court cases with large inconsistencies.

"But I have to be careful," Rick leaned in. "I want consistency in terms of approach. Two kids who do the same thing often should get very different sentences because of who those kids are and their backgrounds . . . there are all kinds of factors that should warrant a different sentence in one case than in another kid's case. It's also difficult to deal with judges who often have very different approaches to the law."

"How do you change that?" I asked.

Through appealing cases, Rick points out, and through formal and informal judicial education.

"I think it's surprising how isolated judges are from one another. Some judges aren't as social as others, and only once or perhaps twice a year do they attend some formal training in a workshop or conference. Judges have to deal with so many issues coming from so many sides that it can't hurt for judges to speak more informally among themselves. Judges should—and do—take part in regular professional training so they get a sense of how the youth justice system is operating. In this way, judges can offer judgments with a little more consistency."

As our conversation continued, I recalled the judge who suggested that in the case of youth crime, the consequences for their law-breaking should come within three weeks or the kids will disconnect from the court's cause for punishment. Rick pointed out the flip side to the judge's philosophy.

"As a defense lawyer, that delay usually works in your favor. The only time it doesn't work in your favor is when your client doesn't permit it to work in his favor. Delay between the criminal act and the sentence is always a wonderful opportunity for the kid to change his ways, and thereby mitigate the sentence. But what often happens is that in that intervening time the kid commits more offences, so he can make his sentencing worse."

I told Rick how, at various times, I have helped residents write a letter to the judge. Sometimes I questioned the kids about their reasons for wanting to write a letter. Were they trying to suck up and get a lighter sentence? The usual response was, "I want to tell the judge in my own words what happened," or "I want to tell the judge how I feel," or "I want them to know my intentions for my future." I also pointed out that this might be a way to show the judge their attitudes towards crime, the victim, the system and society. Rick agreed that these youths' letter-writing attempts to reveal their sincerities showed at the very least that the kids had contemplated their actions. "Anytime you can get a kid to sit down with pen and paper and put his mind to what he's done is a good thing."

"What have you learned about juvenile justice, and what are your thoughts on the system?" I asked him.

"You don't get out what you don't put in," Rick said, getting down to the nitty-gritty. "You don't get good behaviour from kids by teaching them badly or by treating them harshly, and I'm not talking about jails. I'm talking about parenting and institutions and the community." He believed putting hardcore kids in jail didn't change their ingrained behaviour. "My own view is that the only thing that is going to make significant difference to the hardcore offender is the clock, the calendar, the passage of time."

He added that there often comes a time when kids stop behaving the way they've been behaving because of age and maturity, plain and simple. Also, probation officers and correctional officers can help a young adult to gain some insights into their behaviours and possibly, help them change their ways. A probation officer once told Rick that the only thing that would change a kid's behaviour is a one-on-one relationship with an adult that resulted in the kid learning from the adult's 'pro-social' conduct. Being able to form honest and trusting relationships with adults who have the kid's best interests in mind can have a profound effect on a young offender's rehabilitation.

For this reason, Rick said, the system ought to permit and encourage those kinds of mentoring relationships to occur because that's probably the only really effective thing that can happen to a troubled kid, whether it comes from good foster parenting, from staff who go out on a limb, volunteers who hang out with kids, or from programs that offer positive opportunities. And then at some point, this 'pro-social' behaviour becomes more influencing on the kids' decisions than their anti-social behaviours.

RAW VOICES VIII

Letter: "Gary"

Although pleasant for most of his stay at Juvie, Gary assaulted one of our staff. He wrote me several years after he had moved on in the system. The year is 1981.

You might have heard that I'm in jail again. I'm in the Big House for 28 months in a pen [penitentiary] called Drumheller [in Alberta]. It's not too bad of a place to do time in I guess. It's finally dawned on me that I can't and don't want to spend any more time in jails. I was doing 16 months in a provincial joint until I escaped. So I guess I kind of asked for it.

My mother finally found me. I met her in January of '81. She flew out to see me while I was in Fort Saskatchewan [a provincial jail near Edmonton]. I like her from what I know of her. And she's asked me if I want to come and live with her when I get out. I don't really know her all that good. I know that it's too late to be much of a family relationship.

On finding religion while incarcerated:

I think only hypocrites become religious while they're in jail. Most of them only do it for their parole (up here anyways). Well maybe I should try it before I put it down, huh?

I'm going to settle down and have a taste of the straight life when I get out.

And get out he did. It's been quite a few years since I've heard from Gary.

Chapter 19   Speaking from the Bench

"What the hell is a judge doing sitting on his or her ass from a bench four feet above them looking down with the notion that he or she can somehow do good?" says the Honourable Mr. Justice Wallace Craig, retired from Vancouver's skid row courtroom at 222 Main Street where he presided as a provincial court judge for twenty-six years.

It was shortly after his retirement when I sat down with Judge Craig to ask him questions about his profession. I'm from the old school of good manners and social protocol and have always held judges in the highest esteem. By the nature of their position, judges are somewhat removed from ordinary folk on the street. I was more relaxed when I saw that Judge Craig had dressed in blue jeans and a dark green flannel shirt for our lunch meeting in North Vancouver. My apprehension disappeared as we introduced ourselves and I felt comfortable with him as our conversation unfolded. His thoughtful replies to my many questions impressed me and I found his blunt honesty refreshing.

Fairness and the guts to look a man or woman in the eye and pronounce a sentence are innate to this man; they are necessary attributes for any judge in order to serve the law well. Judge Craig's energetic desire to express his thoughts on the justice system and the ills of society has been captured in his own book, *Short Pants to Striped Trousers*.

Although Craig was a criminal court judge dealing with adults, not young offenders, he faced many young adults who had already experienced the youth justice system or who had managed to slip by it. Judge Craig had the perspective of seeing where some kids ended up after they got too old for youth court.

We began our conversation by discussing the lack of discipline in today's school system. We discussed how in the private school system the administration requires parents (and perhaps their children) to sign a contract that sets out conditions the students have to abide by. That means with that signed legal document the administration can kick a kid out of school if they catch the student using drugs or liquor or even if the teachers or principal find out the kid is having sex. It sounds harsh, but the kids know from day one that an agreement is in place that outlines the rules, and the consequences they will face if they break them. Judge Craig and I talked about how the same kind of contract agreement should have to apply to kids in the public school system so the same standards (of following rules and accepting consequences for their actions) are instilled in all young people around the province.

Judge Craig raised a good question: how can you operate a school without discipline? What can a principal do when a child confronts a teacher and says, "Screw off!" or "Go to hell!"? Nowadays, parents are more likely to come into the school, confront their child's teacher and threaten to sue. The judge has seen this kind of reaction from parents whose children have physically pushed or punched a teacher, but his advice to teachers isn't what you'd expect.

"I've talked to some teachers about this and I've explained that self-defense is allowed—if they get pushed around by a student, if somebody punches at them, they can punch 'em back!" But you can't go beyond that, advised the feisty judge. The teacher cannot just take a chair and floor the kid—that would result in firing and lawsuits, something students are well aware of.

Judge Craig also noted that with graduation also comes additional bad behaviour on the part of the kids. "The kids go out and do wild things because they say this is the last time they can do whatever they want. So what does that tell me?" asked Craig. "It tells me that when kids become adults and they've gone through four years in high school where testosterone is running freely and girls are capable of having children, they have all of their own preconceived ideals that set their own standard. Then when the kids make that transition from high school life into adult life, they carry some unrealistic baggage with them. This time in youth's lives is a very egocentric time. For many, it's 'Me first' and 'I set the rules on the road.'

"If the parent wants to stop the egocentric progression from the four-, five-, or six-year age," said Craig, "they have to do it themselves, the school can't do it."

Although school administrators are responsible for the students for a large portion of the day, they are still bound by so many laws that instilling the children with a real and tough sense of responsibility is nearly impossible these days. It's up to the parents to take the kids away from the television sets and computer games at home and teach them respect and responsibility.

"Then when I look at the justice side of it," said the judge as he enjoyed a fresh fruit salad between comments, "it's not for me to know what the prosecutor and the defense lawyers say in court, but I just know that what the judges are trying to do, struggling to do, is to persuade. I don't know how else they can deal with people who are dangerous, dangerous people—mostly men but now increasingly more young women—and I suppose maybe I'm wrong in this, but I think violence is more dangerous than drugs.

Either one is a hell of a big problem."

Craig has always been of the opinion that judges are really just instruments of a legislation that assumes judges can persuade young people to change without making them accountable.

"Permissive judging . . . 'permissive' . . . anything that is permissive in my mind is going to destroy the hope you might have for any kid. If there's no accountability . . . and I don't know if there's any real accountability because accountability in adult life and everything else is based on two things: not wanting to be shamed among your neighbors and peers for doing something that's wrong, and secondly, fear. There's an element of fear in law-abiding people that isn't there in people who choose to scoff at the law—there's no fear in them."

I tossed a question on the table, curious at what the judge's reaction would be to why we allow our present-day tolerance for selfish, egocentric, rule-breaking kids.

Judge Craig recalled an earlier time when historic events had a strong impact on families. "That's rooted in the last fifty years of the twentieth century. The Second World War was a watershed and whether we like it or not, Canada had a class society. It was the well-to-do who believed that the rest of the population was the lower class, not realizing it was mostly men from the lower class who fought in the war. Following the war, more opportunity was available and an emphasis was placed on catering to children, and the road to egocentricity was started."

Judge Craig used his own experience as an example. "Some of the things I did in the time I was thirty-one to say forty-five, when you're in that real aggressive male period, I wouldn't have wanted my mother to know about—whether I was chasing women or whatever the hell I was up to. I wasn't breaking the law but there were certain things that I didn't want to be shamed by—especially as a lawyer. [If a guy invited me to a stag party] I'd say, thanks fella, but I just can't afford that because the cops could come and see me, a lawyer, there."

As Judge Craig noted, that would have been bad for his professional image, and that kind of professional and personal responsibility is perhaps lacking today. I suggested to Craig that he was behaving according to values taught and lived by his parents. He agreed. The judge's candid comments and honesty were most refreshing to hear, and I found myself recalling similar times in my own life when a good value system, modeled by my parents, kept me in line.

"Do you think there are legal consequences that judges could use, but aren't using?"

"Yes," said Craig. He elaborated that judges have the opportunity at hearings to either keep someone in jail or let him out on bail. "Being deprived of your liberty—like at a bail hearing—that's the most discretionary role that a judge can play. Judges can either let them out on bail or say no, you've got to stay in jail. It's a helluva shock to people when they're told they're not getting out just because the word on the street might be 'Oh yeah, you'll get out on bail.'" Judge Craig added that he gets furious when judges say, I'm giving you one more chance. "You should have been told when you got your bail that that was your last chance and you don't get another one. If you screw this bail up, you'll hear two words: detention order."

"Were you ever in fear for your life?"

"No, but I'd look at a guy I was sentencing to jail and I'd think I'm damn glad I'm not the sheriff because that's a hard guy to hold down. When you're a judge you take the chance when you send someone to jail that you will see the criminal goin' nuts and he starts to struggle and get away from one sheriff and another one comes in to help and then you have to press the button for more sheriffs to come and slam him down on the ground. I have a normal level of fear in me but I'm also stubborn enough to look them in the eye and to say, you're not getting out!"

During his time on the bench Judge Craig wasn't afraid to issue a sentence, but he noted that judges were as human as anyone else and can sometimes err on the side of leniency.

There are violent criminals, even within the youth court setting, and as Judge Craig points out, a seventeen-year-old girl or a sixteen-year-old boy can be real tough. Judge Craig said he doesn't call them boys or girls anymore—they're young men and young women, and they can be very dangerous to society. He believes young offenders need stiffer penalties for their crimes.

He brought up the case of fifteen-year-old Jeremy Vojkovic who sexually assaulted and murdered Colleen Findlay, a thirty-nine-year-old mother of three, in a quiet suburb outside of Vancouver. The boy was sentenced in adult court in 2004 and the judge gave him a life sentence with eligibility for parole in seven years. As part of the sentence, the young murderer was able to spend the next three years in a youth custody centre before being transferred to a maximum-security adult prison. "He's walking around with that light sentence," said Craig, "and now he's in among other young inmates and he shouldn't be. I can't believe the young man isn't bragging about himself to the other kids."

Craig continued to say that judges who work with young offenders sometimes act like social workers. Despite knowing what is right from wrong in terms of the law, some judges maintain the belief that somehow they can have a positive influence on an offender by being understanding. He thinks the system needs judges who are in the middle ground who can be hard yet still show some understanding and mercy.

Judge Craig pointed out an example of the necessity for some judicial sensitivity. He had sometimes been frustrated by judges who were not flexible with how they formed conditional sentences. For example, sometimes young offenders are honest with the judge and will say that they will not be able to conform to certain conditions of a probation order, but then the judge will say, that's too bad, I'm still giving you these conditions. Craig said this was the wrong approach because it was clear the offender would break the conditional sentences.

I agree with Judge Craig. When young offenders know that they will not comply with conditional situations while on probation and have the honesty to admit that to the judge, then I think the court should recognize the request; especially when the young offender is willing to comply with an alternate consequence. This is an example of a young person showing insight and taking responsibility for their behaviour—is this not what the system is all about?

"How do you feel about sentencing people to jail—are you able to sleep at night?" I asked Judge Craig this question on behalf of a friend of mine, the mother of two teenage boys.

"I go to sleep in ten seconds!" he said immediately. He could not think of anybody who he had sent to jail who did not deserve to go there, yet he revealed, "I've stayed awake thinking about cases where I've made a mistake." He said there was always the court of appeal if an obvious error needed addressing. "I think more people should criticize judges." Judge Craig was open to criticism—from both the general public and the media—provided it was objective and informed.

Of course, appeal procedures within the court system offer

another kind of criticism of a judge's statements or decisions.

I personally observed many court sessions. In one situation, a judge criticized a judgmental error made by a person who had provided a surety—bail—for an accused. The chastisement of the error was fair. However, the sarcastic and insulting comments made by the judge, in my opinion, were very un-judgelike. This judge knew nothing of the kind of person he was or what his behaviour record or personal behaviour with offenders constituted. Judges are known usually for their thoroughness in gathering all the facts when they make a statement or position or judgment. Basing comments on a ninety-second 'sound bite' was wrong. The comments seemed to serve no purpose, did not further the discussion, and—I thought—tainted the respect and believability of the image a judge should project.

Judge Craig discussed the case of provincial court judge David Ramsey of Prince George who pleaded guilty to sexually assaulting the very children who appeared before him in his court. Associate Chief Justice Patrick Dohm imposed a relatively light sentence. Craig speculated on what the judge could have been thinking.

"Well he's sixty-some years of age, he can't do time because the inmates would do this and that . . ."

Craig said Ramsay was treated like a Roman Catholic priest who pretended to be devout and religious and believe in God then use his power to take advantage of and abuse young kids. "Once a sociopath, always a sociopath as far as I'm concerned, so Ramsay should get what he deserves: maximum penalty. And anyone else who [takes advantage of] young Native kids or young teenage prostitutes should get a severe sentence too because the damage to those young people is immeasurable." He said in these cases where people of power abuse youngsters, the justice system can't ever compensate the victims in a way that would bring them back to normal when they'll not remember the abuse anymore — that is why the maximum penalty for the offender was necessary.

"How do you feel seeing a fellow judge go down like that?"

"I was just astounded," came Judge Craig's reply, "and then I was disgusted and then I was angry at the fact when he did go down he didn't stand up and say, 'I'm guilty and I'll accept my punishment.' Rather, what he did was attempt to make a plea bargain."

According to Craig, plea-bargaining only benefits the accused and harms the justice system. He points out that prosecutors have a choice to have an easy day if they offer or accept a plea bargain. They could agree to drop an aggravated assault to a common assault in a case against a man who beat his wife and withhold pertinent information from the judge. But Judge Craig would warn them, "I'll go the hard way. I'll say we're going to trial, no bargain, we're going. Plea-bargaining is the STD of the justice system!"

"Would you like to have more resources available for sentencing options dealing with young offenders?"

"Only in connection with drugs." Judge Craig said. "Kids have got to have places where they can go to a halfway house or some kind of place where they can get detox treatment. It can be within the jail system or outside the jails, but it needs to be available."

My interview with Judge Hubbard was to take place in his office in the courthouse in Victoria. When I arrived, security ushered me to the judge's chambers through two locked doors and an almost endless maze of hallways that reminded me of the old youth centre on Pembroke Street. Red carpet and oak panels instead of concrete walls decorated the route this time, but the irony of having security escort me brought a silent chuckle to my mind as I followed the guard down the long judicial corridors to the brass plate inscribed with J.M. HUBBARD.

Our last face-to-face contact had been at the old youth centre in the late seventies. It had been early one Saturday morning when I answered the front office door to a gentleman asking if he could use the phone because, he said, "I think I've triggered the alarm in the court house next door!" This stranger was very polite and pleasant, and he seemed a little embarrassed. He used the phone and as we waited for the police to arrive he introduced himself. "By the way, I'm Judge Hubbard."

Now in his office twenty-five years later I reminded Judge Hubbard of our first meeting.

"Yes, I remember that," he laughed.

In starting the interview, I asked this family court judge about his feelings on being involved in the youth justice system.

"Generally good," Judge Hubbard immediately responded. He did have some reservations about the sluggishness of the system and the lack of program options in dealing with youth. He agreed with me that sooner is better when giving youth their consequences, but it's the crowded courtroom schedules that could prolong a decision for months.

As I looked around his office at all the law books, Judge Hubbard commented that despite the bureaucratic setbacks in sentencing they have all this: the library of texts dealing with the process of law, access to all the procedures imbedded in the Youth Criminal Justice Act, and the Charter of Rights to guide judges and the courts.

Our meeting focused on the effect of the government's laws on the judges who have to interpret them. Like Chuck Cadman, Judge Hubbard thought the Youth Criminal Justice Act needed to be simplified. Hubbard admitted that he was not a politician—he carries out the laws created by the public representatives, and the changes and improvements of the laws starts with the members of parliament.

"Are judges too lenient?"

"No." Judge Hubbard went on to explain that people needed to understand all of the factors involved in sentencing before making a judgment on the system. He said that today a decision regarding a young offender would usually be progressive. The judge would be sensitive to what has occurred in the child's life up to that point and keep that in mind when deciding a sentence for the crime as prescribed by law. Hubbard also believed a strong rehabilitative component, especially for younger offenders, needed to be recognized in any sentence while keeping in mind that the overall protection of society must be respected.

Judge Hubbard emphasized that every opportunity for redirecting the young person's behaviour in the community must be given in every sentence. As Judge Craig had mentioned, Hubbard said that when the public or the offender disagrees with any of these sentences the appeal process would be available to them. Judges do make errors from time to time, and there are remedies for that. "But once again," said Judge Hubbard, "we are at the mercy of the creators of the law: the politicians."

Judge Hubbard mentioned that more sentencing options would be a great help for the courts as long as they are authentic, viable, responsible, and appropriate program options of a rehabilitative nature for young offenders.

Judge Hubbard is familiar with the new emphasis for restorative justice. It's been around for many years, quietly working behind the scenes with youthful offenders, but has only recently come to the public's attention, and he reaffirmed that those programs will need more funding and political support in order for the restorative justice model to develop to its potential. He pointed out that with the incorporation of the YCJA into the youth justice system, judges have looked more at diversion programs for young offender sentencing options because they keep young offenders away from the schools for crime that youth custody centres seem to be. But according to Judge Hubbard, at some point after two or three failed attempts to redirect a youngster's behaviour through diversion programs, incarceration is necessary, especially if the crime is more serious.

Hubbard knows that he tries his best when he does his work. He said he hasn't received too many letters to the judge, but he is open to them and welcomes the youth's participation, and sometimes they do affect his decision depending on the contents of the letter and the attitude with which the kid writes to him. He said he likes to know the child's feelings about what he or she has done. He likes to know their attitude towards other people, and with these letters he is able to gain an insight into the person before he decides on his or her consequence.

Chapter 20   The Other Professionals

Gord Irving, Manager

Over coffee in the Greater Victoria Boys and Girls' Club, I spoke with Gord Irving, another veteran worker of the juvenile justice system. In the early eighties, Gord started his career as a corrections officer in the old Juvenile Detention Home on Cold Harbour Road in Victoria, before being transferred to the Metchosin camp that became Coastline Challenges.

Gord is now the manager of Youth Justice Programs for the Boys and Girls' Club, overseeing the twenty-six-day-long Coastline camp, the daytime Nexus program where kids work on a farm in Metchosin, the Intensive Support and Supervision Program (ISSP) that is similar to the one run from the Victoria Youth Custody Centre, and other programs for the rehabilitation of young offenders. Gord is also involved with youth in conflict at the John Howard Society, the YM/YWCA and a number of street church organizations. He explained that at the Boys and Girls Club, the mandate is to provide an opportunity for young people to engage in the community while being supported in a positive and healthy environment. Kids that are involved in the BGC get to look at themselves as positive contributing citizens, and are acknowledged for all of the good things they do.

"Where do these kids come from," I asked Gord, "and how are the kids directed to the BGC?"

"They come on their own or by order of the courts as a way to serve their probation," said Gord. "A young person can come into our services at age thirteen and stay engaged with us for the entire time of their adolescence through housing education, drug rehabilitation, detoxing, and we will support him or her through that change. We're one of the few Boys and Girls Clubs in Canada that provide this broad spectrum of intervention. It's our belief that these kids are part of a healthy community and we need to work with them as with every other family—we have a part to play in the change cycle."

Gord said his greatest concern with the current system is that it operates from a punitive (or punishment-based) perspective that is in isolation from the community. "It needs to operate in an integrated way, for services to the community and the family," he said, and then added it was his goal to make the youth's sentences incorporate well with community life. It was for this reason that he worked for the Boys and Girls' agency and not for a direct government employer.

"There have been huge changes in the kids because I think we look at them differently now. When a kid walks through the door we say, what can we do for you? With that question we try to understand their assets and deficits; it's more of a restorative justice model that looks at the person as a whole person."

At camps like Coastline, kids can take control of their lives and learn skills that weren't available to them before in the city or in youth custody centres. Because of this experience, there is a greater chance of the kids finding work in the fishing or logging industries. But, I wondered, why would a kid want to work or want to learn these skills?

According to Gord, the kids find wilderness camps and day programs exciting and dynamic. Every moment is new and different and the camps support the kids in their efforts to create change through activities in outdoor settings. They get to see their success and opportunities in little ways by cooking a meal, paddling a canoe or seeing a whale.

Gord chose the outdoor setting as the ideal environment in which to work with kids because it is less structured and so there's more opportunity to work with them on an individual basis, rather then always making them conform to the rules in an institutional setting. Staff members live with the kids 24 hours a day for the 26-day program then get time off, as opposed to doing an 8- or 12-hour shift at a typical youth custody centre and then handing the kids over to another staff member. Gord explained the outdoor camp structure emphasizes the value of making a positive connection with a kid as a result of working closely with him or her.

Another big reward for the kids, and of course for the staff, are the graduation days when moms, dads, probation officers, and even judges come to the camp ceremony to witness the depth of feeling the kids have for their experiences and to their commitment for change.

We talked about the current trend in youth sentencing for restorative justice, which is featured front and centre in the Youth Criminal Justice Act. With this justice model, the judge may choose to have offenders sit down, face to face, with their victim to begin a process that will begin to change their violent behaviour and begin a healing process between the two people. Both parties must, of course, agree to participate in the process. The sessions are conducted by professionals who mediate and supervise the encounters and, through these intense sessions, the offenders are forced to face the impact of their crimes.

I asked Gord about programs such as working on ships at sea, farms, and ranches and military apprenticeship programs but he said there were very few of those opportunities available.

"There are a large number of kids out there who aren't being serviced because they don't fit the profile and that's a real concern of mine because we have lost a connection to a larger, silent number of kids."

Gord explained the importance of early intervention for these kids who are getting into trouble. By the time at-risk children reach adolescence, they are acting out with significant violence, causing death or severe beatings.

Gord went on to list some of the early behaviours which can be harbingers of the problems to come. They include impulsiveness, a lack of understanding on the part of the child of how their actions affect the environment around them, cruel mistreatment of pets and violent behaviour beyond the usual roughhousing common in children. Intervention should take place at the first signs of violence. But according to Gord, the intervention should be on an integrated basis, incorporating the efforts of parents, teachers, social workers and criminologists. The cost of this approach would be far less expensive that the cost of incarcerating youth in custody centres.

"Treat the person as a whole person, not as a segment," Gord said. "When we engage in zero tolerance, we engage in zero thinking!"

Gord observed that the core to creating a positive, well-rounded foundation for change in young people is by finding them at least five healthy relationships with adults, whether they be parents, teachers, soccer coaches, aunts, brothers, judges, friends, or correctional officers. I asked him his reaction to the usual, knee-jerk media response to youth violence: "Lock 'em up and throw away the key!"

"I think that's a great idea," he replied, "as long as the person with the key is on the inside, and the kid's on the outside!"

"So is there a place for Juvie in today's society?"

"Sure," said Gord, "there's a place there to support change, to provide a respite from their peers, families, and addiction issues. I see the institutions, at least here on Vancouver Island, working to break out of punitive intervention, and working towards a healthy change. I see it in the way they hire their staff, the training, and how they bring that to the community. Until we place more value on those kids and the staff in the prisons who try to bring about change, the harder it will be to break out of the cycle."

"What was the worst experience you've had working with a kid?"

"When they die," said Gord.

"Best experience?"

"Lots. That's why I'm still doing it. To watch kids stand up and acknowledge their success—that touches me."

Although we have approached our work with young people from slightly different stances, Gord Irving and I share many of the same opinions. His attitude is refreshing and inspirational to both me as a retiree, and to young men and women coming into the field. He has an understanding of both the big picture of government and the legal system, and the unique, small pictures of real emotions experienced in the day-to-day, face-to-face interactions with the kids. Gord's actions and excitement offer young people leadership, life alternatives and a career path that can lead to success and personal satisfaction.

David John, Juvie Teacher

As long as funding permits, the services provided to kids can be as varied as the kids themselves. One of the more important service programs within Juvie is its education program. When I started at Victoria's Youth Custody Centre there were two programs: television and basketball, and the basketball court only had one hoop! There was no school program. There were no arts and crafts, woodworking or physical education classes. Kids need to be exposed to as many of the trades as possible in order to find their niche. They also need the essentials of counselling (in behaviour and anger management, violence prevention, drug and alcohol addiction, and spirituality), and of course, they need an academic education.

David John is a special education teacher, instructing many grade levels at the VYCC, and he agreed to offer some personal insights to teaching in a jail for teenagers. First, we spoke about what it is like to work with youth who have committed horrible crimes. Dave remembered one boy who was convicted of murder.

"When I had found out the details of what he did I was repulsed and it became very difficult to work with him. I didn't want to have anything to do with him but you try and do your job as best as you can," said Dave. "I've worked with other kids who have murdered, and you get to know them and you see all the handicaps they've faced in life and you learn more about the circumstances [that led them to where they are]. But nothing justified what this boy did, and I have also learned that nothing justified what was done to him by society and his family."

Dave explained that for the next four years he worked with that young man and watched him blossom.

"He wasn't being neglected or abused any more, but then the public looks at what he did and they say 'Hammer the bum!'"

The boy's childhood led to him becoming a violent young offender and it proved to Dave that the government needs to intervene in abusive family situations at the earliest possible stage.

"Otherwise we have two victims," he pointed out.

I asked Dave what was his greatest concern about the youth justice system.

"The system seems to be more intent on hammering these kids than on getting them straightened out."

Dave recalled that when he started at Juvie, staff told him to keep the kids safe from each other, and then maybe, just maybe, the staff can deal with some rehabilitation. Dave could understand that although education was important, security was a priority in Juvie. He saw that the staff did a pretty good job of keeping the residents safe, but the teacher in him asked, what was he supposed to do when he saw a kid only six times in the classroom in two weeks—with each of those classroom visits lasting approximately 90 minutes?

Not only did Dave need more time with the residents, he also needed (just as the students needed) a reliable school structure so he could deal with kids who have learning challenges or disabilities like attention deficit disorder or fetal alcohol syndrome. However, with constant demands on the kids' times for court appearances, nurse calls, psychologist or psychiatrist appointments, and probation officers or lawyers requesting visits, Dave faced many stumbling blocks in achieving his teaching goals.

As Dave points out, when these kids can make it to class they have an excellent opportunity to learn. As class size is a big factor in political debates these days, compare the 30 to 1 student-teacher ratio of a regular high school classroom with the average 6 to 1 ratio in a youth custody setting. This cushiony youth centre ratio may look good to regular public teachers until Dave brings up one of his worst experiences in a youth custody centre.

"I looked around and thought, there are seven of us in this classroom—six kids and me—and there's only one person in here who hasn't murdered someone, and that's me! Watch yourself!"

Better than the current youth custody centre classroom ratio would be the one-to-one student to teacher ratio. Dave said "You can make gains, huge gains" when you have the chance to teach privately since the Juvie kids require an extensive amount of teacher attention.

Dave added that the kids in the custody centre also have an advantage over students in the public classrooms because at least in Juvie's controlled environment they have a regular diet, are not on drugs or alcohol, and get regular sleep. Dave sometimes felt like an overpriced babysitter in situations where a resident would come to the school and be released within three days—before Dave could even start an assessment on the kid's learning needs.

A sensitive teacher, Dave is careful to avoid embarrassing a kid in front of his peers. This is a vital character trait as often the kids in Juvie are working below grade level for their age or are handicapped with learning disabilities. Some kids are afraid to let anyone know they are unable to read.

"What's the feeling among your fellow teachers about teaching these kids?" I asked Dave.

"They are here because they like to help children. Each, in their own way, wants to do something for the kids," said Dave. But he warned that teachers can get jaded after fifteen years or so on the job because they've seen their own ideals shattered so many times.

One of Dave's better experiences at VYCC was working with a boy who could not read well. Dave asked the student to tell him his classroom needs in a few words on a small piece of paper. The boy started with "Washroom please" and "I need more paper please." Later, the boy's sentences grew longer as he and Dave began to read together more. This simple teaching process was important to the dedicated teacher. "That was very, very satisfying. Remember, these kids have had a history of failure."

Our conversation turned as I asked, "What would you say to a new teacher thinking of working in a custody centre?"

David answered honestly by saying that first he would let a new teacher know that teaching in Juvie was the most boring, most rewarding and most intimidating teaching job he's had. Juvie typically scares young or inexperienced teachers away. He advises to "be a teacher somewhere else first to get a picture of what a regular classroom is like in a regular school, whether it's an elementary or high school. Practice your teaching skills. Learn how to teach in a school that's got all the support systems. When you really want to push yourself then go into a special education environment. If you look at some of the literature about correctional education, they say the worst thing a manager can do is hire the novice, the young innocent novice."

"Why?"

"It's a hard educational assignment," Dave replied. "For me, the job of working with these kids boils down to how I work with the kids. I know when to push them, and when to back off. It's the ability to teach any lesson for any of the range of subjects with absolutely no warning."

Dave would like to see the centres offering more programs, more materials for the trade programs and more funding for qualified staff. One of his greatest frustrations is the shortage of teachers in the Juvie school system.

I asked him how he and other teachers deal with violent students. He said if a kid starts to act out of line, threatening the safety of the teacher or students, the teacher has to call for the line staff to remove the student from the classroom. Dave has had to do this many times, and sometimes the physical removal of a kid involved two or three staff members and the shift supervisor. These disruptive residents would stay in their rooms for the remainder of that classroom period and would lose some free time later in the day as a result of their behaviours. However, rowdy residents were always welcomed back into the classroom as long as they understood that certain behaviours were not allowed and would be punishable.

Despite these experiences on the job, Dave reflected, "Sometimes I think custody centre teaching is safer than a regular high school. Teaching friends of mine in Alberta have had some very unpleasant experiences with students in the hallways of their schools, and it appears very little can be done by way of consequence or punishment for kids' bad behaviour for fear of legal repercussions on the teacher and school board. I'm sure there are similar occurrences in schools everywhere."

I have a lot of respect for youth custody teachers. They perform a challenging job with great skill and patience. I've spoken to enough ex-residents, long after they're out of the system, to know that they still think well of the Juvie teachers who first discovered how to teach them, and they recognize their dedication with a single comment, "Juvie teachers were the best."

Mickey Webster, Senior Correctional Officer

Tough, upfront, 'flat-lander' (Prairie boy), intelligent, insightful, fair and compassionate all describe Mickey Webster, a VYCC shift supervisor whose official title is Senior Correctional Officer. On a rotating shift basis, Mickey is in charge of the staff and responsible for the centre's residents. After hours, he is the representative for the VYCC director and has the final word in all matters concerning staff and residential interaction including being the deciding factor in admitting residents to the facility.

When I interviewed Mickey, he thought about the improvements made with the youth justice system since the Youth Criminal Justice Act came into effect.

"I certainly agree with the philosophy behind it," he said.

In Mickey's opinion, jail should be one of the last options considered by judges and police when faced with a law-breaking teenager. He believes the system is moving in a direction away from the old attitude of "lock 'em up and throw away the key" and towards diversion and alternative programs for young offenders.

Mickey said that when he first started work in juvie, the philosophy of his training supervisors incorporated security and control. This old boot camp philosophy with the emphasis on the rough and the tough was believed to be the most suitable for treating young offenders. Nowadays, the youth justice system acknowledges that each kid is different and has specific needs.

"Staff members see themselves more as youth care workers," said Mickey. "If a kid does something wrong, you hold him accountable, give him a consequence and in the meantime, try to build a relationship with the kid."

"If I could change one thing," said Mickey, "I'd have the government spend a fortune of my tax dollars, and I'd gladly take a 5 percent increase in my taxes if they would take the money and identify the kids that were at risk before they're born and send in [intervention] staff."

He realizes how impossible that idea sounds—especially the latter part. He has kids of his own so he knows the stresses of parenting, and can easily imagine what it would be like if strangers came into his home to question his parenting skills. However, Mickey believes there should be some kind of structure in place within dysfunctional homes to take away the chaos that brings kids into government custody in the first place.

"That [intervention] might go a long way in breaking the cycle I think."

Mickey's focus turns from radical changes in government policy to the new VYCC in Victoria that was completed in 2002.

"This new facility has had a positive impact certainly on every one of the staff who works there and definitely on every kid who comes in there." Problems that were daily occurrences at the old location on Pembroke Street vanished. He can now walk through the resident wing in the late evening and hear none of the yelling or banging that went on every night for fifteen years in the old place. The 'open design' construction of the new building has had many positive effects on both the staff and residents. Another factor for his co-workers' new ease is that there are fewer kids being incarcerated, mostly due to the new YCJA.

Ann Churchill, Probation Officer

Ann Churchill has been a probation officer in Victoria for nearly thirty years. These days she is responsible for a fewer number of kids as a result of the YCJA which diverts more young offenders to volunteer groups and agencies in the community that run on a restorative justice model.

Ann remarked that this emphasis on community programs seems to have dramatically reduced violence because youth who commit a serious offense are far less likely to commit a serious offense a second time due to the consequence of having to face their victims. Of course, the face-to-face conference cannot happen unless both sides are willing to meet. Ann gave me an example of this restorative justice model. The police caught some kids who had painted graffiti on parking signs. In addition to curfew and a fine, the kids' punishment included the clean-up and restoration of the disfigured and damaged signs.

As far as being a probation officer goes, Ann said, "I think it's one of the best jobs. I enjoy coming to work and I like my colleagues."

Through the youth probation system, Ann gets to meet other support people like those from the Boys and Girls Club, the custody staff and the social workers. For Ann, a probation officer is like someone who goes around like Santa Claus. "Who sees who's been naughty and who's been good," she laughed.

Ann described her role as being a case manager who makes recommendations to the court and acts as an interpreter between the laws and the youth.

"What do you need in the job that you don't have?" I asked her.

Ann would like the authority to dispense bus passes or team memberships for clients rather than making them wait for their requests to go through various levels of bureaucracy. She would also like to see more openings in treatment centres so that youth at risk don't have to wait for the attention they desperately need. She recalled some good words of advice for probation officers that a senior officer had told her when she first entered the field: "Don't overreact."

RAW VOICES IX

Poem: "Of the World"

Death, killing, hurt and pain.
Air pollution, acid rain.
Friends, Greenpeace, anti-warists,
Fighting for our dead rain forests.
Anger, hate, afraid, sad.
Right, wrong, good, bad.
Suffocating in turmoil,
Toxic waste beneath our soil.
Politicians evil laughter
Nuclear warheads, the day after.
Armageddon, Judgement Day.
The final outcome, who's to say!
I can't take it anymore
Too many people just don't care.

Chapter 21   Youth in the Community

Cops & Kids

"Cops and kids—like loggers and tree huggers, they're good for each other!"

I sensed a kind of "I wish I didn't have to do this" feeling from some of the police officers admitting young offenders to Juvie. Not always and probably not the majority of times, but there seemed to me to be a certain compassion present among the officers when dealing with troubled youth. Teenagers under arrest sometimes exhibit the most obnoxious and insolent behaviour known to man! Most officers are very patient and tolerant but there can be times when a kid gets slammed around. The youth's anger abates once the formalities of admission are completed and the police leave youth custody centre.

The kids seem to understand that Juvie staff had nothing to do with bringing them in. Policemen have befriended kids and made a significant, even a profound difference, in a young person's life. Policemen's children have been residents and youth centre staff have also had to deal with their own children in Juvie.

Police officers with several years of experience working with youthful offenders do not see much change in the kind of kids they deal with today compared with kids twenty or thirty years ago but in one RCMP officer's opinion, a lack of fear and absence of respect are two of the most noticeable differences. Municipal police and sheriffs also voiced similar opinions. Values are different today. Emphasis on the worthiness of courtesy, respect for others, good manners and earning what you own have been replaced with taking what is wanted with no concern for consequences—an example of the egocentric personality referred to by Judge Craig.

One RCMP member recalled times during his youth when his parents confronted him on a particular issue, and he was left with the fear of their chastisement and temporary rejection. He feels that today's youth care little about the consequences of their bad behaviour.

One constable made reference to kids demanding their rights in ways that were unheard of several years ago. I asked another officer if he was ever frustrated or pissed off with the YCJA (Youth Criminal Justice Act). Yes, many times, was his reply. The new Act emphasizes diversion, which the officer observed had always been available to them. However, the lack of programs severely hampers the effectiveness of the good intention of the legislation. It is also more difficult to have a young offender placed in custody under this Act. Violent offences are the most common admission criteria today, according to one Mountie's experience.

Corrections staff are peace officers while on duty, and have many of the same powers of the police. Youth custody staff members do not carry firearms or any weapons while on duty. Handcuffs are available to us, but are not carried while in most centres. Staff members providing medical or personal escorts out of their centres sometimes use handcuffs or shackles.

Police presence is a deterrent. Cops on the beat—regular, consistent and available—offer a community good value for the money spent and are just one more plank in a platform of dealing with youth and the community at large. A police officer encouraged me to continue my information presentations about Juvie to school students. Our paths crossed at my grandson's school, and he expressed support to me with the words, "I'm glad you're doing that. Keep it up!"

One of the men on our staff took a year's leave of absence to work for one of the local police forces. At the end of the year's secondment, he returned to his position at the youth custody centre. The main reason given for not continuing with the police was his frustration with a system that leans too far in the direction of offenders' rights and leniency. A personal choice, obviously.

Several other men and women have moved to various police forces, and have found satisfying career paths. Juvie is often a stepping stone to the service-oriented helping professions. I applaud the initiative and personal drive in the people who have passed through Juvie over the years, and for the friendships developed in the process. There is mutual support and a common goal between the police and youth centre staff. I feel enlightened to have been a part of that unique scenario.

A Social Worker's Perspective

"I would appreciate your presenting—in a non-identifying way— any part of this that you may use."

Friends since our high school days, this social worker and his wife stand tall among the people I admire. He has given me permission to share a very personal side of his family's life—the adoption of an infant aboriginal boy. So many of the children who come to Juvie have experienced troubled family backgrounds but this story reveals what is possible when a loving, healthy family raises a child with good intentions and love.

Family relationships such as this one, is what keeps youth away from centres like the Victoria Youth Custody Centre. In the following, the father shares his insight on adopting a child from a different racial background, on the reasons people adopt, and on the long-term effects on both the adoptee and the adoptive family.

"Our motivation to adopt was based on a couple of factors. First, we had two children of our own, both girls, and we wanted to have a boy in our family; adoption would allow us to specify the gender of the child. Secondly, we were willing to adopt children of aboriginal heritage, and we thought we would have a good home to offer such a child. Our preference in applying to adopt, therefore, was for an infant aboriginal boy.

"We picked up Jack [a pseudonym] directly after his discharge from the hospital at five days of age. The girls had been involved in preparing to receive another child into our family and were excited as we were when we picked him up. The history we were given was that his mother was Métis and his father was Ukrainian. He quickly became a part of our family, which was reinforced when he had to go through major abdominal surgery at a few weeks of age.

"Jack's ways of dealing with those around him was very different from his sisters. They were very verbal, always wearing their feelings on their sleeves. Jack was always much more introverted; he was unlikely to volunteer comments or participate readily in conversations, and when angry or upset, would tend to withdraw and become silent so that it was difficult to know what was going on with him. This became a parenting challenge for us as we tended to be verbal 'talking' people. We were never sure whether this difference was a matter of gender (females do tend to talk earlier and more), a matter of genetics, or even a matter of place in the family (i.e. youngest, only male child, etc.). It is a difference that has continued through to the present.

"Another difference between Jack and his sisters was his learning style. They were verbal learners who absorbed ideas by reading, listening and discussing. He was much more of a hands-on learner who could be tremendously inventive using Lego blocks and Dinky cars and other three-dimensional toys. In school, academic subjects were a challenge for him, but he loved practical subjects like shop. As parents who are academically oriented, we often had to adjust our ways of dealing with him, and oftentimes were surprised by how he accomplished similar objectives in very different ways.

"A striking example of this was his way of managing money as a teenager. All of our encouragement about drawing up and following a budget fell on deaf ears. When he got his own car and had numerous cans of gas in the garage, we learned of his method of budgeting—he would put a can of gas in his car when going out with his friends for an evening; when the fuel level in the car got too low, either his friends had to chip in to help pay for getting more gas or they had to go home!

"Jack's aboriginal heritage became an issue during a couple of phases in his growing-up years. When we were living in a Prairie city with a major aboriginal population—noted for significant racist attitudes against aboriginal people, we learned through his sisters that when there were disagreements between Jack and some of his friends, he would often be put down by being called names even more derogatory than 'dirty Indian.'

"He never complained about this and when asked about it, he would just say that they didn't mean it. Some years later, he was physically assaulted without provocation, which we felt might well have been racially motivated. Again he did not blame this [on racism]. He has never admitted that racism is something that has been an issue for him.

"At the same time, he has never expressed any interest in tracing his heritage, even though we have indicated our support if he wished to do this. Jack's appearance is not obviously aboriginal — his dark colouring is actually more Latin in appearance, which may have minimized the degree of racism to which he has been subjected. We could have done a much better job, however, of exposing him to some specific aboriginal customs, practices, celebrations, etc., so that he would have had some very specific matters in which to have pride.

"During his late teen and early adult years, Jack had a couple of brushes with the law. Both of these were related to intoxication. On one occasion when intoxicated, he broke into the house of a friend's parents and took their car with the intent of driving himself to wherever. He was immediately apprehended and held in police cells until I could pick him up. The next day I accompanied him to the family's home where he apologized and offered to make restitution for the damage done. The legal matter was referred to a community justice committee who worked our arrangements for him to provide a written apology to the family and to confirm that full restitution had been made. This was the end of the matter so he was left without a youth criminal record and with an effective lesson on consequences for irresponsible behaviour.

"I would make an observation about the criminal [youth and adult] justice system. I recall as a child myself being caught in an act of unintentional property damage. A friend and I were throwing rocks when one that I threw went through the window of the home of the school caretaker. We took off immediately, but I was unsuccessful in hiding this from my father. When he learned about it, he immediately marched me to the janitor's home to apologize and make arrangements for me to pay the costs as quickly as I could gather the money from my allowance and from doing extra chores. The matter was resolved without any involvement from the police or the criminal justice system. In the similar circumstances involving my son, the police became involved, referred the matter to juvenile probation services who in turn referred the matter to a community justice committee, and who were able to work out the same final resolution as my father had done directly with the victim (the janitor).

"As a society we have complicated matters. The good thing, however, is that society is trying to move beyond the punitive criminal justice process back to individual responsibility and procedures for holding our families and ourselves accountable. After several years out of school (following high school graduation), Jack decided to pursue further education in aircraft maintenance engineering. His previous struggles with academic work disappeared as he pursued a matter that was of interest to him.

"The relationship with our son continues to be less intense than we would prefer. He lives two provinces away, making regular in-person contact difficult. We have accepted and come to value the different type of relationship we have with Jack. Our love and caring for him is as strong and committed as it is with our daughters. We believe that his love and caring for us is also strong and committed. We have had to learn that his and other people's aptitude and ways of functioning are different. In learning to recognize and deal with that, we have become better and stronger as individuals and as a couple. We feel truly blessed to have had and to continue to have him as part of our family."

Restorative Justice

The following section was written by Kelly Orr, a Victoria merchant who experienced restorative justice first-hand.

"If you believe, as the foremost thinking mammal on earth, that we are somehow placed upon this rock to consider only oneself, only participating in a society as a single individual instead of a collective group, then these paragraphs will be of no relevance to you. If you believe that we must conduct ourselves as one, as a group helping each other to further the means of all in society; to act as a family, as one cultural group, then this is an important read.

"It has been my pleasure recently to be involved in what I would consider a community event that helped society as a whole. It took time, patience and involvement when one could have just chosen not to, but the outcome far outweighed all of that. I was asked as the victim of a crime to participate in a program that has evolved over decades. The program is called restorative justice.

"As the victim of a crime I was called by a representative of the restorative justice program as part of a diversion effort through our local municipalities' police department. A young man had committed a crime against my property and it was suggested to me that instead of this young man going through the regular justice system as a first offender, restorative justice would hold a circle discussion with the victim, their supporters, the perpetrator, and his support group—in this case, his parents—the arresting officer, and a facilitator.

"My initial thought took me to a place that scared me a little. Do I really want to meet this person face-to-face, what about the time involved? How could this affect my family? I was informed

that it was totally at my discretion, and given time to consider it. Pondering the issue, I thought to myself how great it would be to actually be able to tell the person who did the damage how I felt about it, how it affected my life — my family's life. I also thought that if this person could see how it affected us, it could maybe prevent further instances. I decided to be proactive and participate.

"A date was set with the understanding that the perpetrator had also agreed to participate. Upon entering the room the evening of the circle it surprised me how uneasy I felt. It was strange to be introduced almost casually to someone who had created thousands of dollars worth of damage to my property. I was introduced to everyone including the meeting directors and the officer involved. I have to say it was comforting to have him there. I was also introduced to the family of the offender.

"At this stage the facilitator and her assistant made it clear that there was a procedure to be followed, but that they were in no way there to counsel or participate in any way, other than to guide us through the procedure. This simply meant that everyone would get a chance to speak, that it would be done in order, once around the circle, with no interruption, then again for responses, and then there would be a forum at the end.

"As the victim, I would speak first. I found myself looking at a young man slumped down in his chair with his hat on sideways and arms crossed. My conversation started soft, and my explanation of damages and how it affected me seemed to come out easy. As I progressed, though, I seemed to be talking to a void and before the end of my talk, I found myself yelling my displeasure of the actions and attitude of this young man. He slowly started to sit up a bit and he started to look at me while I was talking, and something seemed to get to him because he removed his hat.

"Then around the circle we went: the officer, right in character, forceful, letting the young man know how lucky he was to be sitting where he was, and not in jail. The mother cried and talked about family problems. The father cried and talked about his disappointment. By the time we came round to the offender he was upright in his chair crying and apologizing to everyone. The transformation was surreal. It was like a punk turning into an adult right in front of us.

"Once we all had our say, and apologies were made, there needed to be an agreement made for reparation of the damage done. The reparation was discussed by everyone. The first thing I needed, and asked for, was a promise from the young man that he would never do this to anyone again. He sat up straight, looked me right in the eye and promised he would not. Then an agreement was made that the young man would work around my property, repair the damage, and pay for the damage. I almost felt sorry for the young man, as it seemed the reparation part far exceeded the damage done, and he had no monetary way to pay for the damage. At this point, the officer asked the boy's mother if there was anything of value the boy had that could help pay for materials to fix the damage. The mother said, not really, the only thing he has, that he cares about, is his skateboard. I really have to say I felt awful at this point, and wanted to just pay for the supplies myself if the work was going to be done, but a point was going to be made here, and it was past the stage of me stopping it.

"Begrudgingly the young man agreed and his father made him go to the car and get his skateboard. I thought he would just leave and not come back. He came back with the board, and looking straight at me, not mad or upset but almost with true understanding, he handed it to me. I wanted to cry. Strange.

"At the end of the circle, snacks and drinks were offered, we arranged dates for the work to be done (the dates were immediate) and we had open discussion. This went very well. We all had to sign a contract, which was written up by the facilitator, and the circle part was done.

"The first day the young man was to come and do the work, he showed up on time, and worked all day. He sat and had lunch with my friends and me, and I really believe he started to understand that real people were affected by his actions, families and kids. When we conversed, it was like friends.

"On the second day, he arrived on time and finished the work, and he did it well. I thanked him and we shook hands and we parted, maybe not as best friends, but with the understanding that we were both human beings on Earth and here to help each other, not to try to tear each other's world apart.

"As an afterthought, and because I found myself liking this young man, I phoned the restorative justice program and the parents of the young man, and asked if he could do another job for me if he agreed. I also asked, if he agreed and everyone else agreed, if he could earn his skateboard back by doing this work. Everyone agreed, the work was done, and one of the most satisfying days of my life was when I got to look at this young man in his teary eyes, and hand him his skateboard back.

"It has been a while now since my involvement with this incident but I can tell the reader this. The young man in question was dropping out of school, had no relationship of quality with his parents, and was heading down a road of self-destruction. I still see him now and again and last time we talked, he had graduated, his relationship with his parents was good, and he was working full-time for minimum wage. His probationary period was just about *over and he was expecting a raise. I don't know for sure, but if this slight intervention in a young man's life, a tiny moment in time, a small investment by others, could have possibly turned his life around, don't you think it's worth it?"*

Kelly G. Orr,
Victoria merchant

Chapter 22 Youth Centres

I treasure my visits to centres in Canada, the United States, and Australia that have given me unique insights to the justice system. Internationally, I have toured the Connecticut Youth centre and the Echo Valley Treatment centre (near Seattle, Washington) in the US and the Rangeview Remand centre in Perth, Australia.

In Eastern Canada, I have toured centres in Newfoundland, Ontario, and the Manitoba Youth centre in Winnipeg. In Saskatchewan, I visited the Paul Dojack Youth centre in Regina, Kilburn Hall in Saskatoon, a treatment centre near Yorkton, and the North Battleford Youth Custody Centre. I have met the staff at the Calgary Young Offender centre, and in British Columbia, I visited the Prince George Youth Custody Centre, High Valley Youth Correctional Camp near Kamloops, Vancouver's Juvie at Willingdon Youth Detention Centre in Burnaby, Boulder Bay Youth Camp and Centre Creek Youth Custody in the Lower Mainland, and Lakeview Youth Camp and Nanaimo Youth Custody Centre on Vancouver Island. As of late 2003, the High Valley, Boulder Bay, Centre Creek, Lakeview, and Nanaimo facilities have all been closed because, according to statistics, incarcerated young offender counts were down.

Staff from other centres also toured our facility here in Victoria from time to time, and we've had visits from customs and immigration officials to pick up or deliver juveniles from the States. The military police have been involved in our admissions process at Juvie as well, along with the usual municipal police, RCMP, sheriffs and court officials.

There are many youth custody centres in our country and I certainly have not seen them all, but the international, national, and local colleagues I have met have impressed me. I saw that their integrity and humorous attitude when caring for troubled boys and girls was more than what was "part of the job" and their unheralded, diligent generosity had most certainly changed some young people's lives.

Boot Camp in Barrie

The military regimen of a boot camp north of Barrie, Ontario, is one option for an alternative rehabilitation program but its strict structure was certainly not something that I could work with as a supervisor of troubled kids. The professional staff at the camp treated me with respect despite my being an unannounced visitor—although I carried proper identification of course. They were also interested in Victoria's youth custody centre and we traded stories of our respective work environments.

Here is an example of a typical weekday schedule at the Barrie Boot Camp:

06:00   Wake up, use washroom
06:15   Prepare for inspection of clean dorm and ready uniform
06:40   Inspection
06:50   Physical training (calisthenics)
07:20   Shower
07:30   Breakfast
07:55   Wash up
08:00   Clean up mess hall

08:15   Core program: Personal and group counselling in classroom setting for substance abuse, anger management and moral reasoning

09:30   Drill and ceremony

10:15   Quiet time

10:30   Vocational training in woodworking, mechanics, etc.

11:15   Life skills class in hygiene, health, bill paying, grocery shopping, budgeting, etc.

12:30   Lunch

12:55   Wash up

13:00   School

13:15   English class

14:15   Staff shift change

14:25   Phys. Ed.

15:40   Break

15:50   Math

17:00   Supper

17:25   Wash up

17:30   Homework

18:00   Parade in square

19:00   Laundry, phone calls, feedback from staff, next day's prep, cleaning

20:45   Evening snack

21:00   Clean up mess hall

21:10   Wash up

21:20   Inspection of bunks

21:45   Lights out

The residents adhered to the schedule with a military precision. There was little time for foolishness and mischief during their daily, snappy routine. The staff and 'cadets,' as they were referred to, looked very smart in their burgundy slacks and white shirts adorned with epaulettes. I'm sure the local cobblers were happy about all the boys' marching and parading when they replaced shoe leather!

In the past I have helped three ex-residents from VYCC become members of the military, and last I heard they were still serving. The military choice is not for everyone, but its elements work for certain young people who need a strict program that emphasizes guidance and encouragement. Sadly, the boot camp was shut down in the late nineties after the organization overseeing the camp's operations decided to pursue work with youth in other areas.

The Phoenix Treatment Program

Young sex offenders can find treatment at the Phoenix House in Calgary, Alberta. The Woods Homes Foundation, a non-profit organization based in Calgary, offers the Phoenix Treatment Program to a small group of boys each year. This intensive rehabilitation program has been successful in showing kids how to understand their problems and supports their efforts not to re-offend.

Prince George Youth Custody Centre

Volunteers at the PGYCC get to be involved in a positive and productive way—they use their own educational or personal expertise to actually run certain programs. Many of the volunteers are post-graduate students who have the opportunity to learn as they teach the kids woodworking, anger management or drug and alcohol counselling.

Director Stan Hyatt initiated this endeavour, which has been mutually beneficial to staff, volunteers, the community and, of course, the residents. The students who volunteer are in the final stages of their special education or counselling training and get to see the pages of their textbooks come to life; the kids can relate to the young post-grads; and in turn, the staff have fewer fights and obnoxious behaviours thrust at them.

The Prince George centre staff members were open, professional and very pleasant to my colleagues and I when we toured their Juvie. They made every effort to answer our many questions, showing us all the aspects of their facility. We spent much of our time observing the classrooms, program and activity areas and the staff's workday schedule. There were four living units in PYGCC, not including Bowron House. Each unit could sleep up to twelve residents and was staffed with two staff members on day and afternoon shifts.

Communication prevailed at the Prince George facility. The shift supervisor and the teachers met for a daily briefing before the instructors entered the classrooms. This was a brief exchange, highlighting those kids with bad behaviours and any appointments for residents that might cause them to miss school.

Each week, teachers and staff produced a general class schedule for each unit of kids that included subjects like arts and crafts, woodwork, and gym. As a result, residents knew almost a week in advance what their activities would be. Since school was the primary program, staff expected all residents to be in class Monday to Friday. Kids had to attend school or they were classified as a 'cleaner' and would have to scrub toilets and floors, which naturally the kids considered the least desirable thing to do. Those who misbehaved during class time would lose behaviour and attitude points, be removed from the classroom for that period, be removed from class and given room time, be the cleaner, or lose their television privileges. As a result of this policy, the kids wanted to stay in school.

At the PGYCC, each of the four resident units has its own classroom. At the beginning of the day, the teacher attends his or her respective unit while a staff member escorts the students to the classroom; the escort is a brief and simple procedure since the classrooms are located near the living units. The staff member then remains inside the classroom to keep an eye on the kids' behaviour or stands just outside the room to monitor the hallway. Each class has scheduled times for subjects like anger management, mechanics and library time for reading. At the end of class, the teacher and the line staff escort the youth to their next scheduled area. Staff members then remain with the youth at that particular area to supervise the group, ready to step into action if a situation arises.

Although the staff is careful to arrange weekend activities, kids have the opportunity to organize their own things to do provided they follow certain rules. For example, one unit was planning a barbecue and had to ask permission to use the kitchen supplies. Allowing the kids to organize their own activities boosted their morale and encouraged cooperation.

A nurse would visit the units on a regular basis to arrange medical and dental appointments where necessary. Visits with family members and professionals (lawyers, psychiatrists, counsellors) were also arranged in advance. Family visits were much less frequent and staff tried to combine them with the professional appointments in order to avoid constant interruptions to the centre.

This constant scheduling is a much less disruptive way of life not only for someone leading a program but also for the residents themselves, whose lives outside the jails were most likely chaotic. As we did in Victoria, the PGYCC held kids back from programs when they had to appear in court that day.

Staff morale at the PGYCC appeared to be good. Staff members used a personable approach to manage the residents while they maintained order and control in all areas of the centre. Management and staff exhibited a strong initiative spirit when dealing with any request or task.

Along with spending the day with my Prince George colleagues, I spent one full evening observing the program activities and talking with staff and residents on both secure units. As with the daytime, the staff programmed the evenings' activities—right up to ten o'clock at night. Residents could attend Hobbies (arts and crafts), Gym (run by a volunteer), Chapel (spirituality counselling, run five nights a week), or have free time to watch television or play cards. For each of the programs, a staff member would escort the residents to and from their units while another staff member would supervise those who remained in the unit for lockdowns or early bed times.

Every week, the staff evaluated the residents on a points system based on 'Performance and Attitude.' The kids began their week with a full slate and then lost points for misconduct in each area. Staff felt that being able to give consequences for bad attitudes was very effective in keeping the residents in line because no teenager wants to go to bed at eight o'clock.

A low point level can affect things like a resident's pay rate and bedtime. Every centre has its own system for paying the inmates, but generally kids are paid fifty cents an hour while they are on a work crew and attend school and other scheduled programs. Some people disagree with paying kids while they are in Juvie, but I've seen that it encourages them to go to school and become involved in their rehabilitation programs. And not all of the residents spend their money on personal items; I've seen them give their pay to charity at fundraising events.

I spoke with several residents, two of whom have been incarcerated in Victoria. Both of the ex-VYCC kids and two of the others with whom I talked to liked the PGYCC but didn't entirely like the complicated behaviour points system.

They thought there wasn't enough time for kids to just talk to someone; one said "the staff never has enough time." The residents also thought that staff wanted to control their every move with the strict scheduling. Some of their comments, of course, must be taken with a grain (maybe a pound) of salt, but I've usually found that gut reactions are usually truthful. Judging from their feedback, the youth with the highest ratings liked the points system but the youth at the bottom seemed to find it confusing.

Each unit had a time-out room. Youth could serve their lockdown punishment in their own rooms but if their bad behaviour persisted the staff moved them to the time out room. If they were still misbehaving, they could be relocated to Living Unit #5, an isolated cell away from the four living pods. If residents were in #5 they would be slowly phased back into their unit, starting with maybe an hour per day or with a communal mealtime until they could gradually earn their way back. Staff placed the most serious lockdowns (youth requiring intense observation) in a time-out room called 'Medical Observation,' a cell that was monitored by video from the control room.

Job postings at PGYCC consisted of specialized duties and staff could let the senior management team know if they were interested in working in certain units or areas. Each staff member identified his or her top three choices, and more often than not ended up getting one of the postings, with each posting typically lasting for at least one year. This procedure is also in effect at Victoria's centre.

Staff participation in the centre's operation was very similar to the custody centre in Victoria. The case management, school, line staff and program directors made classification and clinical decisions while line staff dealt directly with the residents' consequences, but the shift supervisor has ultimate authority. On the administrative side, the director of operations and the director of programs would make the staff development decisions.

When it was time for a shift change at the PGYCC, the incoming staff and the senior officer would first meet in the staff room where they discussed any highlights and low spots of the day by looking at the unit reports that were dropped off in the office beforehand. This meeting would last for approximately five minutes, and then staff members went to their posts to complete the shift change with the outgoing unit staff.

The Long Lane Youth Center, Connecticut, and its ISSP

The Connecticut youth centre is the largest youth centre I have visited. When I was there in late 1993, the resident population was approaching three hundred. The large campus was nestled in the green hills north of Hartford and there were many different buildings, both large and small, housing residents and program space. Unique to this centre was its follow-up program—the institutional staff would check up on the ex-residents, appearing at any time or anywhere, for upwards of a year following their release. This program was an example of an Intensive Support and Supervision Program (ISSP) that included supervising the kids' curfews, work attendance, school programs and home or living situations. The program was an astounding success, reducing recidivism (relapsing or bad behaviour) to less than 20 percent compared to more than 70 percent before the program started twenty years before. The staff commented to me that this type of strict and extended follow-up program gave the courts "teeth," the police support, the staff job satisfaction, and the kids a chance for the future.

Treatment at Echo Valley

Echo Valley, East of Seattle, Washington, is a treatment centre for troubled youth. At the time I visited, it was a large, campus-style centre.

Programs included therapy and treatment for many disorders affecting the young people in its care. Some kids there had mental, behavioural or personality disorders, while others were sexual offenders. Echo Valley functioned more as a treatment centre than a place for incarceration even though it did house and care for young law-breakers serving sentences.

New Haven Correctional Centre

The progressive programs for the adults incarcerated at New Haven Correctional Centre, as the name may suggest, offered a fresh approach to the punishment and correction of young offenders. After I spent sixteen hours touring New Haven and speaking with the staff and 'trainees,' as the inmates were referred to, I felt that New Haven was truly a correctional centre, unlike other adult confinement facilities such as the old Oakalla facility in Vancouver or the Wilkinson Road jail on Vancouver Island.

In a system based on learning responsibility in a supervised setting, New Haven was like a Valhalla that offered young adult offenders an opportunity to learn self-discipline, to learn to relate and be respectful to their peers, subordinates and superiors, and to learn the freedom of responsibility. New Haven's belief was that when an inmate could accept responsibility for his actions he has taken the first steps toward correction and personal freedom — this is the philosophy that needs to guide the programming at more youth centres.

Young people need to feel secure, develop meaningful relationships and take pride in their accomplishments. They also need to be nourished and at New Haven, the trainees cooked three regular meals each day. New Haven helped establish the value of work by involving their residents in cooking and housekeeping duties. On campus, residents took on positions as woodworkers, metalworkers, farmers or cooks while senior residents worked in the community outside of the centre. Junior trainees were given rudimentary tasks in the first couple of months after admission but once they'd proven themselves capable, they would be promoted to an intermediate level. As a result of these work programs, the trainees learned valuable skills, developed a sense of satisfaction and learned that, in order to be promoted, they had to be responsible for their own behaviour and decisions. Also, the dormitory setting was the best that I have seen.

Staff members were responsible for training the inmates.

They also guided the trainees towards better socialization and increased self-esteem. Residents expecting to be left alone at New Haven to do their time were in for a rude awakening. The trainees participated in almost all activities, in groups of about thirty; even an evening of bingo and television required group participation. If someone did not want to be part of the group he would lose a privilege or be demoted.

There were also posts that required a lot of responsibility on the part of the trainee. For example, the 'duty monitor' had to count his fellow trainees every hour, and it was his job to report any missing trainees to the on-duty staff. Of course, the staff made periodic random counts as well. Duty monitors who lived up to expectations would learn some on-the-job management and communication skills. Failure to report missing trainees would immediately demote him and extend his sentence at New Haven. Again, the emphasis here was on the trainees taking responsibility for their actions.

How long does it take to form a habit? A day? A month? Three months or longer? I feel that most people need adequate time to form new habits in order to cast aside the old. We must be firm when we teach new work and play habits because it takes time to erase old, unhelpful patterns; that's why time was crucial at New Haven.

After four months, new trainees were really just at the first level in creating effective, disciplined and caring interpersonal relationship with staff and their fellow trainees. This is why I think eight months is a good term for correction—once formed, good habits are hard to break, but first they need time to set.

Also learned from my visit to New Haven was that a group of young adult offenders, following certain ground rules, could successfully manage themselves under supervision. Although it shocked me that this institution went as far as allowing offenders to carry keys, I was pleased that it inspired offenders to be trustworthy. In a system that allows participation and expects responsibility, trust and respect become the unspoken norm, and that's what I'd like to see nurtured in all youth custody centres.

RAW VOICES X

Letter: "Tim

In December 1995, "Tim" was about to finish several months of juvie:

Well Gord I'm gone in a couple of days so I just wanted to let you know that I really appreciate the way you've treated me and helped make a bad situation better, and the way you helped me learn from my mistakes. Well thanks again I'll always remember your good heart.

P.S.   Don't change, you've helped a lot of people and I think you could help a lot more.

Epilogue: The Time Capsule

The original idea for a time capsule belongs to Mickey Webster, the VYCC shift supervisor I wrote about earlier in the book. He approached me and asked if I would be interested in putting one together, considering that I was the oldest fossil around here!

I and two videographers from Camosun College's graduating class of 2001 were given unfettered access to the old centre located at 1125 Pembroke Street in Victoria. Videographers Krista Lomax and Lee Vanderbyl filmed the first documentary over the fall months of 2001. Mickey and I then decided a second video would be shot to showcase the centre's new building at 94 Talcott Road. This second video, videotaped by Morgan Waters, also a Camosun College graduate, was shot in a more casual 'walk-through' style.

Both VHS videos were included in the time capsule, along with letters, photographs and drawings contributed by residents and staff. My years at the centre since 1976 gave me access to photographs, shot from the inside, some of which I had taken myself over the years. These were also placed in the time capsule.

There was no agenda—political, financial, policy or otherwise—to serve. Our goal was to present a picture of life inside a young offenders centre from the perspective of those who lived and worked there, by capturing the conversations of residents and staff on film. I was happy to contribute my experience and 'insider information' to the making of the videos and the creation of the time capsule.

It is certainly my hope that the opening of this time capsule in the year 2042 will be enjoyable, revealing and entertaining to those who peruse its contents and view the videos. I believe our activities as shown and revealed will truthfully reflect our sincere efforts to work in a professional and effective manner with youth offenders during the latter part of the twentieth century up until 2002, the time we completed the making of our time capsule. A bronze plaque sits atop the concrete-enforced capsule in the courtyard of the new centre at 94 Talcott Road.

New technology, discoveries, attitudes and philosophies will shape future policies in regards to caring for teenagers, a very difficult segment of our population. I can only hope that many of you will benefit from the knowledge that I and many of my colleagues have gained in our careers at the Victoria Youth Custody Centre over the years. If I can sum up my work with teenagers—

Listen.

Gordon Cruse
Staff
Victoria Youth Custody Centre
1976–2002

Gordon Cruse had a long and satisfying career working with young offenders as a youth supervisor at Victoria's Youth Custody Centre for 26 years. A foster parent since 1973, Cruse completed two years of pre-med studies at the University of Saskatchewan. He also worked 14 years in radio, both on Canada's west coast and the prairies as well as a year as a rock 'n' roll DJ and newsman with Radio Caroline, the first of the offshore British radio pirate ships. Now retired, he lives in Victoria, BC.